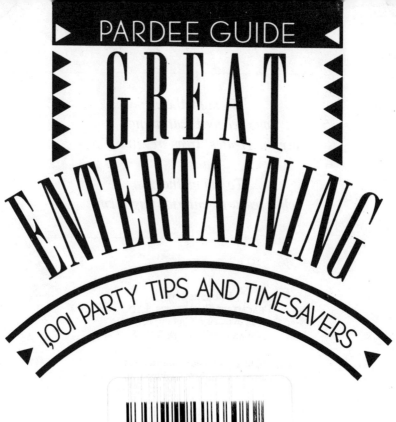

PARDEE GUIDE

GREAT ENTERTAINING

1,001 PARTY TIPS AND TIMESAVERS

BETTIE BEARDEN PARDEE ·

PEACHTREE PUBLISHERS, LTD.
ATLANTA

To my father,
who believed that friends
are the greatest treasures in life ,
and
To my mother,
who treasured entertaining them

Published by
PEACHTREE PUBLISHERS, LTD.
494 ARMOUR CIRCLE, NE
ATLANTA, GEORGIA 30324

Cover design by Lytton Design
Cover illustrations and interior illustration by Cynthia Carrozza
Interior design by Candace J. Magee

Manufactured in the United States of America

10 9 8 7 6 5 4 3 2

Library of Congress Cataloging in Publication Data

Pardee, Bettie Bearden,   date.
    [Guide to great entertaining]
    Pardee guide to great entertaining / Bettie Bearden Pardee.
        p.   cm.
    ISBN 1-56145-001-4 :
    1. Entertaining—United States. I. Title II. Title: Guide to
great entertaining.
BJ2021.P25   1990
395'.3—dc20
90-41753
                                                                    CIP

CONTENTS

An Entertaining Point of View

Growing up Southern is all about entertaining.

In my family, if we weren't planning a party we were re-covering from the last one or looking for an excuse for the next. Anything became an occasion and any reason would do.

But entertaining to us meant much more than just "giving a party"; it was a cherished part of our lives. For we believed that if you really enjoyed people, entertaining became the art of pleasing friends—of welcoming them warmly, of anticipating their needs, of surprising them with something unexpected. In my mother's words, gracious entertaining began with making a guest feel "at home."

I learned very young that gracious living is its own kind of sanctuary from the pressed-for-time lives that we all seem to lead. And when I think of entertaining—the camaraderie of sharing food and drink—gracious to me means the pleasures of dining in all its myriad forms . . . Sunday brunch, Friday night after-theater supper, Tuesday luncheon. It means lingering over coffee, listening to the end of an amusing story or a bit of gossip in a relaxed, intimate setting.

Knowing how to entertain—*graciously* and *easily*—while having **FUN** at the same time, inspires an enviable sense of confidence. With this for you to look forward to, I'm passing along a varied collection of entertaining secrets, practical suggestions, super shortcuts and time-tested traditions. I've also included personal preferences culled from years of entertaining—and even more years of being entertained. I've admired and adapted pointers from these other accomplished hosts and hostesses who all share one thing in common: their memorable parties seem flawless—and appear effortless.

Oh, yes . . . They also share one other very important attribute—*they have learned how to be guests at their own parties.*

And that's what this book is all about . . .

Taking The Guesswork Out Of Being A Host

I like to think of this book as a present you give yourself—a quick peek at all the necessary details of party planning and giving—"telling it all" in a clear, no frills style that respects the demands on your time.

❦ You can skim the book and add hundreds of useful hints to bolster your own repertoire;

OR

❦ You may make this your party guide book—keeping it on a convenient shelf and hunting up the tips for entertaining in small spaces, the explanation of a party rental contract, suggestions for hostess gifts;

OR

❦ You might use it as a scan-n-plan workbook, taking advantage of the handy checklists, pages for your own notes, charts for guest list and menu planning, sample instructions for the caterer;

OR

❦ You may see it as a teaching tool to tell others how you wish something done—washing the fine crystal after a dinner party, the maximum height of a table centerpiece, the attire for the bartender;

OR

❦ You can use it as a reference for managing party professionals and support staff, with time-honored tips for smooth working relationships.

GREAT ENTERTAINING is designed to demystify and symplify so *you* can get on with the **FUN** of entertaining. After all, when the party starts, are you going to be a guest or aghast?

GREAT ENTERTAINING

SECTION
1

INSIGHTS ON ENTERTAINING

INSIGHTS ON ENTERTAINING

Who doesn't welcome some guidance through the practical ins and outs of party giving?

While entertaining is simple if you have the know-how, it can be challenging if you don't. The following is a collection of pearls of wisdom, practical observations and time-honored truths to help you put that personal signature on your own entertaining style .

Wit and Wisdom from Successful Partygivers

On Entertaining

☙ The most gracious of gestures is to help a guest feel "at home" in your home. Everything should contribute to a feeling of warmth, welcome and camaraderie.

☙ Entertaining should be a reflection of your lifestyle, dressed in party clothes.

☙ A good party is the product of details played upon details. Everywhere one turns, it's details that are remembered, details that set something apart.

☙ Guests who feel pampered won't know, or care, whether you spent three weeks or three hours getting ready.

ANECDOTE

Send guests home with a little something — mini bottle of home-made herb vinegar, personalized poem, special potpourri, tiny paper flower nosegays to use or tuck away with fond memories.

---

*L*ead with a Theme

A theme's pluses are many. Not only does a theme give an imaginative impetus to the party, it provides focus during the planning stages and offers a means of involving guests from the moment their invitation is received.

Opportunities for inspired themes abound—a season of the year, a time-honored recipe, a favorite color. Themes can be keyed to personal events—a visiting friend, a move to or from a different clime, a refurbished kitchen. Or they can play on humor, divulging suppressed desires. A theme is a party's personal signature, lending that irrepressible sense of occasion.

❦ Unexpected or unusual locations add immeasurably to a party's spirits; sometimes the location itself is reason enough for the party.

❦ Feeling at ease with entertaining comes with practice. Create reasons, look for opportunities to entertain, don't wait for an occasion that demands it . . . and find yourself caught off guard.

On Being a Guest

❦ A favorite guest will always be at the ready to help out —watching for "strays," being an engaging conversationalist, anticipating a host's predicaments.

❦ Send flowers or a note the next day, even if it's just a witty postcard.

❦ Leave quietly, and without any fanfare, if it is necessary to depart early. A round of big good-byes too early in the evening throws a damper on a party; later in the evening it tends to break up the gathering.

❦ Don't call the host during those critical 30-60 minutes before the party starts; be considerate and ask all questions days, or at least, hours ahead.

❦ You're not just window-dressing; you have a responsibility to contribute to the success of a party.

On Being a Hostess

- The accessible and endearing hostess feels an obvious delight and generosity in her role, assuming a style that is relaxed, efficient and pampering.

- Knowing your own comfort level means that you can then plan and invite accordingly.

- Plan effectively so that you can be cool and collected when guests appear. Few things are more unsettling to guests than the impression that their arrival has been preceded by a household commotion.

- Stick with what is familiar. Be kind to yourself and don't try a new recipe, new hairstyle or new room arrangement for a party.

- You want guests to feel: **privileged** to be there; **pampered** by your anticipation of their every need; **pleased** that *you* are enjoying your own party.

- Don't forget to introduce guests to each other, always passing along a little snippet of information to encourage their conversation.

- When suggesting attire, be as specific as possible, especially if the guest has never been in your home before. For not only are they "making an appearance," but thoughtful guests realize that their choice of attire will pay a compliment to the host.

- Don't let a situation persist that will embarrass a guest, be it lack of sobriety or spinach in the teeth.

- To be an effective and satisfied host requires the ability to care and share, perseverance, a touch of showmanship and a healthy dose of vitality.

- Anything slightly non-traditional will bring out a sense of adventure in guests, almost as though in being unorthodox yourself, you have sanctioned it in them.

On Food

- One cardinal rule: Never run out of food at a party. Remember, quantity needs will vary with the makeup of the guest list. Strangers will be more likely to concentrate on food, while friends will talk more, and eat less.

- Don't feel compelled to serve "fashionable" restaurant food. If guests wanted Soufflé Rothschild or Oysters Bienville, they'd opt for reservations around the corner.

- Just prepare the BEST of whatever you're serving and success is guaranteed (your grandfather's favorite chili, that first dessert that you mastered as a bachelor, the pheasant pot pie that celebrates your husband's annual hunting trip).

- It's helpful to note *both* cocktail and dinner time on an invitation.

- Resist overworked presentations that look showy and contrived. The emphasis should come from the surroundings, with attention focused on the setting, the plates, the accessories.

- Consider menus that are versatile enough to be served hot or at room temperature and can translate from sit down to informal buffet.

- Because of their flexibility, buffets are an ideal party format. An entire menu can be prepared ahead, then put out to be available for most of the party. Plus, buffets can be tailored to any budget and expanded at the last minute, if need be.

SHORT SUBJECT

Add an interesting note at a dinner party, while making the preparations easier on you—

Serve one or two courses away from the dining room (soup or appetizer, coffee and dessert). With this format, you can be tending to final dinner preparations while guests are enjoying their first course or providing them a change of venue after dinner.

Pay attention to details in the accessories that can enhance the pleasures of dining:

▼ Serve bowls of fresh grated cheese, or croutons, with soup.

▼ Provide a fresh nutmeg grinder or powdered sugar shaker with appropriate desserts.

▼ Offer two types of sugar with after-dinner coffee— amber rock crystal as well as white granulated.

▼ And for a final treat . . . pass *"just a bite of chocolate."*

The Four Secrets of Entertaining

1. STOP

over stretching, overreaching, over scheduling.
Resist lofty ambitions that haven't undergone a trial run.

2. LOOK

for shortcuts, time-enhancers, labor-saving tricks.
Don't underestimate the time and resources required
   and
Don't overestimate your capabilities.

3. LISTEN

to experts with tips on everything — from how to clean the house in record-breaking time to dealing with stress and pre-party nerves.

4. YIELD

to the lessons in each entertaining situation.
Learn what you want to repeat.
Learn what you want to do more of . . .
And learn what you will not do again.

Where Do You Start?

By answering these Six Simple Questions

1. WHY?

Why are you having this party? Is it to celebrate a milestone or personal event, or to honor a person or a holiday? Is it an impromptu gathering or a business, civic or social obligation?

2. WHAT?

What type of party will suit the above occasion—cocktail, seated buffet, tea, barbecue, dinner dance? What theme will tie it together? What attire is appropriate? What will *you* wear?

3. WHEN?

When should the party take place? When should the invitations be mailed, the wine be delivered, the caterer arrive?

4. WHO?

Who should be invited? Who will cook the food, design the flower arrangements, provide the music?

5. WHERE?

Where should the party take place? Where should the bar be set up? Where will you go if it rains?

6. HOW?

How much will it cost? How will the planning be organized? How will the details carry out the theme?

Counting On Your Best Assets

Entertaining is an ART. Polishing up the following will let you count the rewards in time saved and pleasures savored.

Planning and Preparation.
Remember the Boy Scouts.
Planning makes that memorable party seem flawless—and appear effortless.

Imagination and Inspiration.
Imagination is the well-spring for fresh ideas, colorful images, and innovative choices.

Creativity.
The vital ingredient.
Creativity is your personal signature that turns great inspirations into even greater accomplishments.

Attention to Details.
Be persnickety.
A successful party is a collection of well-tended details.

Spontaneity.
Watch out. It's catching!
Stay loose, be flexible, relax and enjoy.

Sense of Humor.
Rx for every hostess.
Plaudits for its remarkable capacity to help keep things in perspective.

Organization.
Organization is an elixir that will calm anxiety, steady the nerves and ward off frown lines.

Prerequisites for Party Planning

Accept time realities—
Budget enough time. Party planning isn't taxing. It's just an accumulation of a lot of little jobs. Break the big job into little ones, each doable with the right amount of time and energy.

Write everything down—
Have notes for your notes. This compels you to be realistic about just what is entailed in a specific project. Note-taking also spares you the stress of having to rely totally on memory, and gives you a well-earned sense of accomplishment as you check off "to-do's."

Know yourself, be proud of it, make an asset of it.
Tailor your entertaining style to your lifestyle. Doing what you do best, charmingly presented and with calm conviction, is far superior to a frenzied and failed attempt at what you think you "should" be doing.

Make flexibility your social ally.
In entertaining, as in life, Murphy's Law will always prevail. The ability to bounce back is one's best defense. Overcome an obsession with perfection and welcome the unpredictable for the spark that it brings to any gathering. "If you can't flee and you won't fight, then FLOW."

Stay focused.
This means don't be indecisive, don't get sidetracked. Keep in mind that distractions are seductive time thieves.

You'll Enjoy Your Efforts More, If You . . .

1. Welcome entertaining as an *opportunity*—to express your individuality, to share your creativity, to extend your hospitality—and to have a good time doing it.

2. Develop an easy-going attitude. Gracious living always conveys the impression of ease.

3. Consider yourself first and plan for a party *you* will enjoy. For only then can you communicate this positive feeling to your guests.

4. Accept that it's better to be kind than to be perfect. Adopt an old French proverb as your modus operandi:
   "La Beaute plait,
   l'esprit amuse,
   la Bonte retient et
   attache."

   > BEAUTY PLEASES,
   > WIT AMUSES,
   > BUT KINDNESS KEEPS YOU
   > CAPTIVE.

5. Practice "attention to details" in your own day-to-day life. (Use special scented soaps in your bathroom, keep bud vases of your favorite flowers around at *all* times.) Pampering yourself with details will put you in the mood and make you an old hand at an important ingredient in successful partygiving.

6. Treat yourself *first* to your own home on the night of a party. Allow enough time before guests arrive to sit quietly and absorb the atmosphere of your party-ready home. Have a first drink with your spouse or friend to christen the room; then move to different areas around your home to observe and enjoy the vistas you have created.

7. Polish your organizing skills. If you're not organized by nature, now is as good a time as any to start. What better reason do you have than to share your leisure time with friends?

8. Don't take yourself, or the party, too seriously. Overcome the erroneous view that the tides of fortune will rise or fall with this entertaining attempt.

Discover Ways to Make It Easier . . . The Magic 10:

1. Look for reasons, themes, occasions to have a party. This "helps" you entertain by providing an impetus and focus.

2. Keep a party journal over the years. Include a copy of the invitation, guest list, seating plan, menu, drinks and wines, decorations, flowers, entertainment, staff.

3. Avail yourself of all your resources: party rental shops, take-away food stores, wholesale flowers and food, friends, spouse, children, dog.

4. Become a voyeur. Look for table-setting ideas in magazines, party favors and surprises in museum gift shops, table and entertaining accessories in thrift shops, color and decorating inspiration in your travels.

5. Use your best for everyday as well as entertaining. Having to take things out of storage, cleaning and re-bagging them makes entertaining a chore.

6. Never underestimate the power of mood. Music, candles and flowers are fabulous party aphrodisiacs.

7. Relax in the fact that there are no entertaining "rules" today. Let individual whims and needs dictate your own personal style.

8. Put your freezer to work for you. Cook with future entertaining in mind; prepare additional quantities for freezing ahead.

9. Plan two parties back to back. With everything in place—rentals, flowers, table set-up, not to mention cleaning and cooking preparations—it makes the second party a snap.

10. Have a back-up menu. Check out your local takeout and catering services, their hours, locations, menus (see pages 47-9, 108).

Remember One Great Truth:
It's **attention to details** that distinguishes the gracious host from just another party giver.

GREAT ENTERTAINING

SECTION
2

WHAT MAKES A PARTY GO?

WHAT MAKES A PARTY GO?

It's a sense of creativity, of fun and the unexpected that makes a party come alive. From Great Beginnings—that warm, personal greeting at the door—to Great Endings, when guests step out of that perfect moment with memories—a party that works is planned to please in every way. Well-orchestrated details, those party ingredients that are both necessary underpinnings and subtle enhancements, are the keys to successful entertaining.

Small or large, formal or informal, unforgettable occasions owe their success to a devotion to details. Here, to get you started, are some details on those details that make a party *go!*

Creative Casting

Guests are not the most important ingredient in your party—they **are** *your party! Have you ever tried to have one without them?*

Many liken the design of a guest list to the planning of a fine menu—keeping a sharp eye on balance, freshness and texture, while seeking out the surprise of a piquant ingredient, color for our visual palates, the accent of delicate herbs.

The friends who honor us should enhance, and in turn be enhanced by, contrast with other guests. The felicitous results? A synergism that results in spontaneous exchanges, a little flirting, laughter and an anticipated sense of discovery.

It's too easy to fall into a routine with the same old standbys and friends who see each other regularly. Guests want to be amused and fascinated—by the colorful politician, the thought-provoking journalist, the witty raconteur—even to the point of not always being in agreement.

$\mathscr{H}$erewith, some pointers on the fine art of assembling a party's cast:

- *Let the occasion guide you* in the composition and character of your guest list.
  - ◊ Is it a celebration of a milestone or personal event?
  - ◊ Have you chosen to honor an individual or a holiday?
  - ◊ Are you fulfilling a business, social or civic obligation?
  - ◊ Or is it simply an impromptu gathering for no occasion at all?

- *Go for diversity!* A party that comes alive boasts an eclectic collection of guests. Mix personalities, ages, professions, personal interests—and idiosyncrasies. Add a dash of spice . . . with someone famous or preferably infamous. *Who your guests share a good time with is as important as the menu.*

- *Invite enough guests* to ensure a congenial gathering. The party space and number of invitees should work in tandem. Too large a space and not enough people, guests feel self-conscious and withdraw; too small a space and too many people tend to overwhelm guests.

- *Need a creative approach* to an eclectic guest list? Start with a few couples and have each invite another couple.

- *Everyone enjoys seeing* someone new and different, so include some out-of-towners or new arrivals. They contribute ingredients highly prized in a guest list—new face, fresh point of view, varied interests, tales from afar.

- *Guests can provide pace* and flow, acting as punctuations at different stages in a party's life (i.e., arriving after-theater for dessert, joining a post-luncheon croquet game).

- *Always try to include* at least one invitee who truly understands the art of being a guest:
  - ◊ They appreciate their responsibility to contribute to the success of a party.
  - ◊ They are witty,

charming, good storytellers and can draw out others in conversation.

◇ They will act as a second host—making introductions, rescuing someone from a bore.

◇ They are always ready to help, anticipating the party giver's potential predicaments.

♦ *When entertaining professionals,* try to achieve a cross section of businesses. This should prevent lapses into dull "shop talk," as well as moot professional questions that may spark sharp debates.

♦ *If circumstances* beyond your control find you with a disparate assortment of guests, structure opportunities for "instant bonding." Dividing people into groups—for a scavenger hunt, cooking contest, sports competition—calls up that old team spirit and attendant camaraderie.

♦ *Necessity demands* that a guest list be homogenous? Too much so? As in a gathering of all plastic surgeons, or car salesmen or investment bankers. "Squeeze in" two or

three colorful couples who can shake things up a bit—or call on a few tried and true friends who can help you energize the group.

♦ *Create reasons* to bring casual acquaintances together. People are flattered when you have looked for an opportunity to entertain them. Let a singular common interest —i.e., collecting Russian furniture, game cooking, study of hieroglyphics— serve as the impetus.

ANECDOTE

Some people like to do crossword puzzles or read cookbooks in bed. One hostess prefers creating "ideal" guest lists, matching brand-new acquaintances with a cast of old friends, scripting just the right mix of chemistries to spark compelling conversations.

As a memory jogger come party time: Keep a running list of new people you meet at parties, old friends you unexpectedly see, business contacts you might not otherwise remember.

♦ *Keep a record* of your party guests lists, including pertinent notes for future planning. This also serves you in hindsight as you recall successful (and not-so-successful) combinations.

♦ *Graceful entertaining* implies reciprocity, but avoid the once-a-year payback party that is often a study in crowd control. This insensitive approach to a guest list only makes for a cumbersome and uncomfortable party. Guests will perceive early on that they were all invited merely because you "owed" them.

Your Memory Jogger List

_____

_____

_____

_____

_____

_____

_____

_____

_____

_____

_____

Tables of Content

An invitation to dine "at home" is a warm and gracious gesture. What makes it a gracious and *civilized* gesture is for this sharing to take place at the table (not balancing a plate on your knee). What guest does not anticipate the opportunity to partake of good food, wine and stimulating conversation, in a personal and intimate atmosphere?

Setting the stage, creating the ambiance that welcomes and embraces the partygoer is the hallmark of an accomplished host. The table affords you the means to create this congenial environment for dining . . . to enjoy the self-expression in mixing and matching china patterns, shapes and colors . . . to play on details to carry out a theme—in the centerpiece, the party favors, your linens.

♣ The table is as much a fashion statement as you are. Don't just set it, dress it thoughtfully. Guests will remember the table decor and ambiance long after they've forgotten the meal.

> **PARDEE TIP**
>
> **Dealing with limited resources—budget or space-wise? Concentrate your creative efforts and dollars on the table. After all, this is where guests will be spending most of their time.**

Going the Rounds

Thin might be in, but round is the choice for party-going tables. Every great entertainer knows that round tables help you

Establish a Gracious Tone: With no "head of" or "end of" the table, a sociable equality is suggested. Also, everyone can see each other without craning and straining.

Change Moods Easily: Floor-length cloths are romantic and also permit a quick change of mood and decor. Additionally, a tablecloth is visually cohesive, whereas place mats suggest boundaries.

Stimulate Conversation: All guests are accessible to each other — no one is limited by odd angles; cross-conversation can take place at any point on the circle.

Enjoy Practicality: A round table can be inexpensively assembled with a lumberyard wooden pedestal and plywood circle. Or, a large collapsible round table can be placed over a simple card table.

Practical Points

● Homemade plywood round tables are not only easy to make, but are also kind to your furniture budget. In choosing this option, instead of a "fine" dining room table, you have eliminated a costly decorating purchase.

PARDEE TIP

Include a felt, or "silence," cloth under a tablecloth to pad wood surfaces.

● Full length cloths for round tables can be inexpensively created from department store sheets (see page 120 for quick tricks with sheets.) Change looks, or create a theme, with the snip of your scissors; then toss the sheets in the washing machine when they pick up any spills. Sheets can become one of your biggest decorating finds, representing as they do every conceivable fashion trend—from Chinese porcelain to English flowers to hunt-country plaid.

SIZE-TO-SEATING RELATIONSHIP

36" diameter = 4-6 people   48" diameter = 6-8 people
42" diameter = 6-8 people   54" diameter = 8-10 people

NOTE: The maximum number for each table size may require compensations (i.e., placing napkin on plate, using only one wine glass, eliminating salad/bread and butter plate).

Table Talk

Successful Seating

Remember! As host you're also the casting director. Always designate where guests will sit, to ensure the fruits of your guest list planning efforts. Successful seating starts with an eclectic guest list whose diversity sparks curiosity and stimulates keen conversation.

Mix those personalities, interests, professions and ages, while keeping an eye on these seating strategies:

✪ Designate a guest as host for each table.

✪ After announcing dinner, if guests are slow to move, start noting where guests will be sitting. Or ask one person to start the buffet line. If it's a large group, don't hesitate to politely "usher" them into the dining room.

✪ Consider ringing a bell to announce dinner. Psychologically, the sound of a bell spurs people to action. (Shades of school days?)

✪ Don't seat husbands and wives together (The old etiquette would exempt newlyweds, but that's why it's old.) And don't seat good friends side by side. (This is boring for them, because they see each other all the time. It also makes for "insider" chatter.)

SHORT SUBJECT

While circumstances may sometimes compel us to make-do, there is actually a charm and sense of fun about intriguing alternatives to serving and dining. For instance, old apartments boast oversized odd spaces that can be turned into instant dining areas—perhaps with a stretch of the imagination (i.e., pillows on a radiator cover for extra seating around a table). The point is that a lived-in room possesses special warmth and therefore gives added appeal when used as a dining area. Conversely, where you do have a separate dining room, make it double for other purposes; when it's not being used for dining, it will have a life of its own.

Remember the thoughtful
Golden Rule-r of 13 inches

▲ **No centerpieces should be *above* eye level (approx. 13").**
▲ **No candle flame should be flickering directly *at* eye level.**

✪ Place cards are a practical assist for a hostess at a small dinner party and a necessity for guests at a larger party. Place cards can cover the gamut from formal—gold-edged or engraved—to informal—a leaf with a guest's name written in white ink.

✪ Don't be locked into "rules" regarding strict ratios of male and female; rather, keep your eye on common interests and conversational talents.

ANECDOTE

A Washington embassy hostess has arriving guests draw colored paper leaves from a bowl. Each leaf is then matched to its counterpart and pinned to a napkin at the table.

✪ To enhance general conversation, keep centerpieces low and clutter off. A table overburdened with glasses, accessories and decorations is distracting. But smaller tables, and therefore closer guests, stimulate conversation flow.

✪ Don't wait dinner for a latecomer. Begin, and let the tardy arrival slip in, starting with the course that is on the table. Out of consideration for all, make as little fuss as possible.

✪ For a change of pace . . . come dessert time, have some guests change dining partners; on the back of the place card write the name of the person with whom they will be trading places.

On a FORMAL NOTE

The most important guest is seated on the hostess's right; second most important male guest on her left. The most important female guest is seated on the host's right; second most important female guest on his left.

Table Etiquette for Guests

❦ Talk to your table partners on both sides of you, not just the good-looking one.

❦ At a table of six or fewer, wait until everyone has been served before starting; six or more, it's impractical to wait or the food is going to get cold.

❦ If in doubt about which utensil to use or how to eat something, "watch the hostess" (presumably if she's serving it she knows what to do with it).

❦ While clearing the table is always well-intentioned, don't voluntarily get up and start removing plates unless the host has accepted your offer. The flow of a dinner party is interrupted when guests break off conversations to head to the kitchen. (In the most absurd of situations, the entire table can end up there!) It is often more appreciated if you stay and help keep the conversation going in the host's absence.

Interesting Sidenotes

❦ In formal dining situations, bread and butter plates are not used; rolls are placed (no butter is used) on the tablecloth, above the forks, or on the folded napkin on the place plate.

❦ In French table settings, it is an old tradition (the better to show off family crests) that forks are set with their tines facing

down and spoons are similarly reversed.

❦ Italian place settings offer no clue as to which utensil to use next, whereas in "American Service," silver is placed in its order of use, starting from the outside working in. And no more than seven pieces of silver should be on the table at one time.

Not enough of one set of tableware for the number of guests invited? Get creative. Combine different sets of china, glasses and flatware at each table.

The Buffet Table

A "seated buffet" meal is a happy marriage of convenience—pairing the elegance of seated dining with serving ease and flexibility.

There are no formal setting guidelines for a buffet presentation, only practical ones:

♠ Place plates, napkins, and cutlery in close proximity to each other.

♠ Pay special attention to the visual appeal in the choice and arrangement of serving dishes and bowls.

♠ Eliminate the feeling of clutter as effectively as possible — consolidate little dishes on one tray; opt for a few larger containers rather than a lot of small ones.

♠ Choose adequate but not overscaled serving dishes. Visually, large mounds of food are less appetizing and more difficult to keep hot and fresh.

♠ Be conscious of sufficient light so guests can comfortably serve themselves.

♠ Leave extra space near a dish that requires two hands for serving.

Table d'hôte

When the dinner is not "at the table," but "on the knee," you can make it less cumbersome by providing your guests with three thoughtful essentials:

1. a "fork, no knife" menu
2. larger-than-dinner-size plates (12" plus)
3. oversized napkins (24" x 24")

or

create "mini-tables" for each guest—individual small trays, complete with place mat and silver, awaiting guests at the end of the buffet.

Decorating with *Flowers*

Many feel that a house is not a home without flowers. For it is these long-stemmed beauties that make a home feel "lived in" and traditionally impart an atmosphere of welcome.

Today, creativity in flower design incorporates the full spectrum of flora—from woodland greenery and moss, to topiaries of dried flowers and berries, to still-lifes of fruits and vegetables, so popular in old Dutch paintings.

Let the occasion, your furnishings, the time of year, style of party, and your choice of tableware guide you in creating with flowers. Make selections to enhance the color of your china or reflect the spirit of your personal possessions. View flowers as accessories, like pearls that adorn a basic black dress. Your choice and particular use of flowers should express you in just the same way as do your clothes and furniture.

Garden Variety Notes

- Keep in mind that, just as with a clothing accessory, decorating with flowers allows you great versatility. The arrangement and the placement can either be used to enhance a possession—as one hostess observed, "I've never received so many compliments on that painting"— or to play down an eyesore by distracting attention.

- Dedicate one spot specifically for flowers, sited so that the arrangement is noticed at once by anyone entering the room.

- Never underestimate the elegant simplicity of a single flower in a simple bud vase. Masses of flowers are not always necessary; the eye is refreshed merely by the sight of one flower.

- Flowers should meld into and complement their surroundings, not compete with them, a task made easier by keeping a careful eye on color choices, scale and container.

- Mixing colors:
On a limited budget, don't mix colors in single arrangements (it takes too long to create a visually harmonious grouping.) *Do* mix shades of one color with one other complementary color for accent. Arrange using *odd*, not even numbers of flowers.

Before arranging:

- Let flowers get a good (at least 60 minutes) drink of lukewarm water.

- Cut stems on the diagonal with a knife and make a small slit up the center (app. 1/2").

- Remove all foliage below the water line.

- Extending their life: Two secrets to remember—
(1) Re-cut and
(2) Change the water, on average, every other day.

Use a 50-50 portion of water *with* a non-diet citrus soft drink. (Sugar gives flowers an extra boost). Also, add 1/2 teaspoon chlorine bleach per quart of water to stop mold.

- In planning a centerpiece for the dining table, be careful with too-fragrant flowers (i.e., hyacynths or ginger) or those that would conflict with the aroma of food.

Easy, Elegant, Economical Choices for Home and Table

Fresh and creative combinations abound when you develop the habit of looking at flora for its individual decorative quality without concern for its conventional context, be it fruit, vegetable, weed or flower. Following are suggestions for accessorizing your party home with the bounty of nature —easily, elegantly and economically.

AROUND THE HOUSE . . .

● Weeds, grasses, bushes, limbs all have their own majesty. Use them alone, or as fillers to dispense with the need for lots of flowers; as a creative option, "plant" limbs in a clay pot (chicken wire covered with moss), twine with ivy and highlight with single flowers (their water vials hidden by clusters of moss).

● Topiaries are easy to make and great assists in carrying out a theme. These small "trees" (ranging in height from 6 to 24 inches) consist of a straight trunk with a ball at the top—made of any selection of fresh or dried flowers, greens, berries, nuts. (see page 121 for design directions.)

● Bunches of small nosegays are effective massed together as one large arrangement during the party; after the party each small bouquet becomes a party favor for departing guests.

● Cut amaryllis provides a dramatic and cost-effective statement when "planted" in the top of a dramatic urn.

● Do-it-yourself flowering indoor bulbs are kind to your budget and almost fool proof.

● Orchid plants cost the same as one or two arrangements and last three to five weeks longer. A good choice for people with little time—there's no need to change water, re-cut and re-arrange, or deal with debris.

- Use individual bud vases at place settings as a "favor" for each guest; or mass single vases on an antique china platter, silver tray or tea table for a centerpiece.

- Arrange a still life of favorite objects (porcelain birds, tortoise shell boxes, art pottery) and highlight with bud vases. Stagger flower heights to complement the scale of your still life objects.

- Use small, laquered paper "art bags," like those found in museum gift shops, and fill each with small bouquets.

- Let a green plot of alfalfa sprouts "bloom" with single flower stems. Or consider a philodendron leaf for a place mat.

- Discover the world of possibilities in the produce section of your local market. Arrangements are very easy to make and while lasting just for a day, they all will enjoy a second life in the kitchen.

- Use hollowed-out vegetables and fruits—apple, pear, cabbage, squash, melon, artichoke—for natural "bud vases."

SHORT SUBJECT

Fruits, vegetables, nuts and berries can become a re-creation of a Dutch still-life painting, complete with half-peeled oranges and quartered melons; a space filler for large surfaces (flowering kale or green cabbages with their leaves carefully peeled open); a complement for flowers (large baskets of mixed berries, with tufts of Queen Anne's lace or freesia peeking up; a mélange of white blossoms nestled among the ruffled leaves of ruby lettuce); and a singular statement on their own (perfect baby eggplants or pomegranates, cut to show the intricate patchwork of their seeds).

For an ethereal effect, spray fruit, flower and vegetable combinations with a water mister to give the impression of a garden's morning dew.

Florists Speak Out

A florist's greatest frustration, presumably the customer's, too, results from miscommunication—he designed what was workable within your budget; you expected "something fuller, lacier, with fewer daisies."

The more common ground that can be established, the better.

Some working pointers:

① *Develop name and price awareness.* If you have fallen in love with long-stemmed French tulips and English cabbage roses, be aware that they are four to five times the price of their lesser garden counterparts.

② *Don't be shy about your budget.* Discuss your likes and dislikes specifically, so you can be comfortable with compromises if they need to be made.

③ *Provide adequate information.* The florist needs to know where the arrangement is to be used; whether it will be seen from one or both sides; how long the flowers must last. In some circumstances you may even choose to supply the florist with your personal containers or fabric swatches. Also, magazine pictures of arrangements or styles that you like will make a big difference in clear communications.

④ *Give your florist enough lead time.* The majority of florist-available flowers are imported from Holland (with the exception of roses and tropicals). Deliveries usually require five to seven days. However, depending on the season and your choices, a florist may need two to four weeks for planning, ordering, delivery time and arranging.

Compleat Containers

Unique and interesting flower containers are yet another example of attention to entertaining details. And with the emphasis on the container, you can be much more flexible in your selections; inexpensive floral choices will suffice.

Searching out the vase or container is a creative exercise of its own. Be on the lookout for shapes, textures, sizes and materials—anything that can hold water or can be lined with a water-tight filler.

Suggestions . . .

▼ miniature liquor and brandy bottles

▼ food and condiment jars—Italian olive oil bottles, French mustard jars, English biscuit tins. (Consumer product companies spend millions on packaging design; they've done all the work for you to enjoy.)

▼ perfume bottles (You couldn't go wrong with an entire collection of these romantic vials.)

▼ pharmaceutical flasks (Clean contemporary shapes for very little money.)

 HORT SUBJECT

Your home cupboard is just waiting to be pressed into service— it's where you might find a pewter beer tankard, majestic silver wine cooler, ceramic pitcher, copper kettle.

And some favorite possessions deserve another look — a precious silver baby mug, crystal brandy snifter, grandma's old sugar bowl. Or an antique box, perhaps one of the most versatile and appropriate floral containers. In any material— warm rosewood, painted tin, engraved silver, hammered brass—a box is effective because it serves double duty both as a decorative accessory as well as a container for flowers. Ideally, the top of the box should be hinged so that when opened (and lined with interesting paper or fabric), it provides a backdrop to your arrangement.

These are the three standbys that no home should be without

❶ any basket that is already prepped with a liner

❷ small glass bud vases

❸ glass globe (8" diameter is ideal) This last is the most versatile. Spray it with color, wrap it with fabric, mount it on a stand, stack a group of them. Glass globes afford flexibility, too, because flowers fan out naturally and need little arranging.

Floral Designers

Consider a "floral designer," rather than a retail florist, for occasions that require more than a simple party centerpiece. Why?

❦ These creative talents design for and around the decor, be it your home or special party location, using flowers as one of the elements.

❦ They make "house calls."

❦ They are often more creative, less likely to have clichéd arrangements.

❦ They order flowers fresh for each specific job, (as opposed to retail shops where larger inventories often get old and tired).

❦ They usually don't have retail shops, which cuts down on their overhead and thus, your costs.

Night Lights

All people and all things *glow* in candlelight. Its romantic mood-inspiring properties are legendary. Just lighting the candles tends to put you in a festive mood, while their peaceful quality compels guests to relax; not a small consideration given the hurly-burly schedules of most people.

And on the table . . . candlelight will do for complexions what only plastic surgeons promise.

Herewith, some illuminating answers to oft-asked questions regarding candles.

When to use?

Candles should not appear on a table before "teatime" (4:00 p.m.) and when present, should always be lighted.

Uneven burning?

A breeze of any kind will cause a candle to burn more quickly and unevenly, and spatter on walls, linens, wood. Be conscious of air conditioning and drafts.

Quick fix?

Place candles in the freezer for several hours before using. This will make them burn more slowly and evenly with a minimum of wax drippings.

Best value?

"Devotional" votives, those sold for use in churches, will burn for 10 hours; beeswax candles (with no animal fat or other ingredients) are dripless and smokeless.

Too hot?

Filling a glass votive with 1 inch of water will dissipate the heat from the candle.

Removing wax?

Placing votive holders or candlesticks in the freezer for 15-30 minutes will cause wax to pop off. Bobeches (2-inch glass rings that slip over candle) catch candle drippings and cut down on wax clean-up.

Insect problems?

Citronella candles are outdoor entertaining boons for repelling insects. Creatively packaged, they are particularly effective around food preparation and serving areas.

Cigarette smoke?

"Smoker's" candles are available in short, thick tins, that will neutralize (though not cover) cigarette and other smoke.

If your candle base is too large for the candlestick hole, warm the lower end of the candle with hot water and trim it with a knife.

Party Dressing

The cheerful play of candlelight mysteriously affects the senses —and makes a room rich in feeling.

Mix your favorite candleholders on a mantle or entry table—tall, short, silver, brass or crystal—to create a fiery dance of shape and texture.

Or search out the creative "fakes"—life-like wax interpretations of everyday objects (from shells to foods) to suggest a theme or enhance a motif.

Some possibilities:

- fruit tart candles massed on a silver tray for non-caloric centerpiece

- wax nautilus and pecten shells for a summer seashore table

- circular angel candles that burn down the center only, leaving a hollow into which a votive can later be placed

- tall, skinny French "sparkler" candles marching atop a cake

- apples mounded in a bowl with tapers (1/4" to 1/2" thick) anchored in the stem of each upright fruit

- large, black Japanese pebble candles to intersperse on a table landscape of real black pebbles and Oriental flower arrangement

- silver or gold candles for an anniversary or holiday events

- and to dress up the outdoors . . . *"candelarias"* (colored paper bags weighted with sand supporting a short candle) to line walkways, porch rails, tops of walls.

But it's votives that get the vote for all-around versatility

■ Enjoy the flattering effect of their subtle, low angle light.

■ Play on their ability to pinpoint light in out-of-the-way spots . . . tuck into a bookcase; nestle among a grouping of picture frames; place inside a cherished bowl in a collection of porcelains.

■ Group under indoor trees and bushes for a natural, uplit effect.

■ Wrap with artificial gold leaves at holiday time, green leaves in spring.

■ Hollow out squash, artichoke, ruffly cabbage as votive containers for the dining table.

■ Use a votive on a clear plastic stake for nestling into flower arrangements.

■ Go for drama! Place a votive atop a tripod of three raffia-tied chopsticks.

■ Finally, take advantage of the innumerable votive holders available—cut crystal, pierced brass, woven bamboo, holiday-decorated glass—to help complete a decorating theme.

Lighting Strategies

❖ Keep lights brighter at the beginning of a party when people need to connect; lower them as people settle in.

❖ Pink light bulbs are the most flattering to skin tones.

❖ Avoid overhead lighting; opt instead for low angle lighting that reduces hard edges on faces.

❖ Indirect lighting (in corners, under plants) is effective because it has a mysterious, ephemeral quality — you know it's there but its source is not obvious.

❖ Use a dimmer whenever, wherever. It will become your most expedient lighting addition, providing welcome flexibility and a range of light levels literally at fingertip control.

❖ Lighting outside a window makes a room feel larger.

❖ Stress strong and adequate lighting in cooking and service areas.

❖ 40-60 watt bulbs provide enough light, while still conveying atmosphere. Over 60 watts should only be used for reading or work areas andwalkways.

EXTERIOR

Landscape lighting deserves attention from both a security and aesthetic standpoint.

❖ Use a professional lighting specialist and investigate all costs thoroughly.

❖ Use only a licensed, experienced electrician, well-versed in the demands of exterior lighting (i.e., water proofing and insulating).

❖ Bushes and shrubs are more successfully lit

than flower beds, which tend to look scruffy and dingy.

❖ Pay special attention to access walkways and rocky or uneven steps.

❖ Consider photocell attachments that react to natural light levels, causing lights to come on at dusk, go off at dawn.

High Notes

Few of us need to be convinced of the power and persuasion of music. (How many times has a song triggered a memory?) But with some thought, come party time we can be more creative than simply switching on the sound system and playing our old standbys.

Music is an important underpinning of any gathering. It's no wonder that seasoned party givers use it to set the mood, pace the flow of the party — and give it soul.

A Few Maxims on Music

❖ Appropriate is the key word. If it is not in keeping with the guest list or the purpose of the party, it can be a liability.

❖ Live music is preferable — a quartet greeting arriving guests, a strolling guitarist during the cocktail hour, a piano player after dinner (whose presence prompts people to sing). But recorded music offers more latitude in selection of songs and volume of sound; plus, there is no dealing with a temperamental musician.

❖ Schedule cassette or compact disk (CD) selections so that a mood change will occur every quarter hour.

❖ Louder music acts as an icebreaker at the beginning of a party, filling the void of guests yet to arrive. But the sound level should be lowered considerably after half the guests are present or conversations will turn into shouting matches.

❖ For a cocktail party, where guests may not know each other, opt for vocal music. Live performance albums, interrupted by waves of applause between numbers, are especially effective, psychologically stimulating a crowd of strangers to mingle freely.

* Come dinner time, lower the volume again (around two on the receiver). Clamorous sound inhibits good digestion and music that is loud enough to be recognizable tempts one to hum along, rather than converse.

* The greater part of the dinner hour benefits from a musical backdrop of solid tonal selections, music that is "unobtrusive"; skip those pieces with overly insistent rhythms or vocal accompaniment.

* Spontaneous music making can be a high point of a party — from guests "playing" their water and wine goblets at the table to sing-alongs around the piano.

* Try to structure opportunities that will prompt people to sing. Singing is special to all of us because everyone can "make a glad sound" in some humble way without any talent.

* Roll up the carpet, or plan ahead for a dance floor, and one good thing leads to another. Dancing just comes naturally when there's a little "fascinatin' rhythm" afoot.

Get in the Swing

There is music available to suit every purpose, every pocketbook and every personality—and a party provides just the welcome opportunity to exercise your imagination. Consider:

String Quartet	Spanish Guitar	Funk
Disk Jockey	Baroque	Swing
Horn Quartet	Chamber Music	Motown
Jukebox	Dixieland	Gospel Singers
Dueling Banjos	Country Rock	Rap
Latin American	Calypso	Samba and Bossa
Steel Drum Band	Big Band	Nova
50's Be-Bop	Folk	Ancient South Amer-
Harp	Reggae	ican instruments
60's Rock	Jazz	
A Cappella Choir	Soul	
Blue Grass	Renaissance	

It pays to search out your own "finds" and to hire
directly. Booking agencies charge markups that can
run as much as two times union scale.

Where to find interesting and
easy-on-the-budget musicians?

❖ Local universities and
schools of music are
happy to provide names
from their music faculty
or student body.

❖ Individual members of
the local symphony, rep-
ertory theater and opera
group musicians are
available also.

❖ The boy's choir of a local
grammar or junior high
school offers an intrigu-
ing note at holiday parties.

❖ Residents of a local retire-
ment home or club are yet
another option, availing
themselves of the luxury
of free time to pursue
what might only have
been a pipe dream in their
business-career days.
Look here for the likes of a
barbershop quartet, Dixie-
land jazz band, group of
ukulele players.

❖ Finally, check out clubs,
pursue word of mouth
recommendations, collect
cards from bands you've
heard in your travels or
partygoing.

Once found, what questions should you
ask? What guidelines should you follow?

◆ Know exactly what kind
of music you want. Being
knowledgeable, and as
specific as possible, will
eliminate confusion and
the chance of unantici-
pated surprises. Visit

clubs, listen to records
and tapes at the public
library, go to music
school rehearsals to
familiarize yourself with
the wide range of choices
that are available.

When using live musicians, be sure to clarify the issue of "continuous music." Five to ten minute breaks per hour are standard in any contract. But you do have the right to decide when those breaks will be; also, that there will always be at least one musician providing live music at **all** times.

♦ Ask the musicians for suggestions from their repertoire and what they feel they do particularly well. This is similar to asking a caterer for a suggested menu.

♦ When pricing the "gig" (industry lingo for "odd musical job") **ASK:**
◊ *What do you charge per person per hour?*
◊ *What do you charge overtime, and when does overtime start?*
◊ *Is there a minimum number of hours that you must play?* (Solos or shorter gigs will often cost more due to the up front cost of setting up, tuning up, etc.)
◊ *What are additional charges?* (ie., travel, parking charges, musician plays an extra instrument or a particularly cumbersome one). These costs will usually apply if you are using union musicians.
◊ *Are there any special situations or requests that I should be aware of?* (i.e., If a piano is required, it is the party giver's responsibility to provide and have tuned.)

♦ Confirm that a band or group you are considering regularly work together (an ad hoc collection of musicians is not recommended).

♦ Preview the musician(s). This is almost an ironclad rule if you have never heard them before. Any reputable musician will have a "demo tape," sometimes even a video; in the case of students, make arrangements to attend a rehearsal.

Don't ask a professional musician, who is also a guest, to perform. If he wants to he will . . . whether he's asked to or not.

◆ Arrange to meet the musician(s) in person to make certain the chemistry is right. Their physical appearance, manners and attitude should be checked out early to avoid uncomfortable situations at party time.

◆ Lastly, book as far ahead as possible and get a contract. Or at least consign your agreement to writing. This should include answers to the questions cited above *and* the terms and penalties for cancellation. On this point, be sure you have individual phone numbers and call to reconfirm.

Your Notes

So What Do You Do For an Encore?

Parties getting a little stale? Tired of the same old musicians, deejay, rock band making the rounds?

Consider some of the following options when the party circumstances call for some live, and conversation-worthy punctuation:

+ "Get personal." Palm readers, fortune tellers, hypnotists provide an opportunity for guests to discover their more private selves.

+ Bewitch and bewilder with celebrity look-alikes, female impersonators, ventriloquists.

+ Amuse your guests with mimes, impressionists and cartoonists.

+ Go for live decorations—i.e., body painted and cloth-draped actors that look for all the world like real marble statues . . . until a subtle shift in pose causes guests to do a double take.

+ With a few strokes of pen and pastel pencil, caricaturists capture on paper a guest's singular features and idiosyncrasies . . . for a great take-home favor.

+ Or consider the face painter, who works his magic directly upon your guest's visage—transforming it into a jungle tiger, monarch butterfly, circus clown.

Just a sampling of what's available from the wide world of entertainment. And don't forget the balloon makers, jugglers, acrobats, dancers, fire eaters, stilt walkers and escape artists.

Great Resources

Great entertainers are masters at delegating . . . which presumes they've developed an enviable roster of resources. Marshalling these party allies becomes another critical component in making a party *GO*.

PRACTICAL PARTY RENTAL SERVICES

Advice from a Jewish mother — *"So rent it!"*

Dealing with party rental stores is one of the few instances in life where you'll actually save money by spending it. After all, when the party's over, what *would* you do if you owned 72 demitasse spoons and where *would* you store that 40-foot tent?

Pointers from your "Party Ally"

Competition is stiff in the party rental business, which is to a host's advantage. Therefore, rental shops strive to distinguish themselves by the level and quality of service they offer. Make the most of your working relationship with this party ally.

Cardinal Rule #1
Allow Enough Time:
Plan way ahead to ensure availability and choice. Rental services' busiest times are May-June, September and Christmas.

Cardinal Rule #2
Educate Yourself:
All party rental stores have itemized price sheets of everything in their stock and "consumer friendly" pamphlets for party planning down to the last detail.

Meet with them in person, visit their showrooms. Selections can vary by store, so it's a good idea to check out two or three.

Cardinal Rule #3
Be Practical:
Plan a party based on *your* desires and *their* available equipment.

♦ Understand clearly the "fine print" in rental store contracts (see page 51).

♦ Review the order as soon as it is delivered, the better to rectify any oversights on their part and last minute needs on yours.

♦ Determine the condition in which you should return rental equipment;

water-rinsed is standard procedure.

◇ Household dish washing and liquid detergents leave a residue which reacts adversely with commercial dishwashers.

◇ Additionally, party rental stores use a strong chlorine-based, industrial-strength cleaning soap that kills all bacteria.

PARDEE TIP

If unable to accommodate your specific requests, a party rental store will usually refer you to a competitor or other resource.

SHORT SUBJECT
The Caterer-Party Rental Connection

If using a caterer, it's to your advantage to delegate the co-ordination of rental needs because:

❶ A caterer is more familiar both with the rental equipment and your specific party needs.

❷ Their personal working relationship can exact favors (rental stores will often make themselves available 24 hours a day, and by beeper, for their catering contacts).

❸ A caterer will not usually apply a markup to rented goods; but if so, it is nominal and well worth it.

Read the Fine Print

If at all possible, avoid SURPRISES. The "fine print" in the party rental business generally covers these points:

❑ **Deposits**
A cleaning deposit is required on some large items (i.e., food preparation equipment such as charcoal grills and hot dog roaster); a non-refundable rental deposit is requested on tents (typically one third).

❑ **Delivery and pick-up charges**
These are based on distance from the warehouse; delivery is to a "mutually agreed upon" *ground level* location.

❑ **The party giver/renter's responsibilities**
These responsibilities cover the period from delivery to the pick-up. They include making sure that the equipment is protected from the weather and is secure from theft.

Three Final Points

① Clearly understand the pick-up time. During normal seasons, pick-up would be the next business day (i.e., Friday night party, pick-up on Monday). During busy seasons, it may be necessary to pick-up the next morning on a weekend—or even after the party.

② Discuss the damage waiver.

③ Review your homeowner's policy. Does it cover theft of rented goods and, or those goods used in locations other than your home?

A Random Sampling of Rentable Items

Party rental stores are a fixture in the planning of any party. Consider the vast range of entertaining needs available to you for nominal charge—from shrimp forks to cotton candy machines.

- ❏ Disposable party goods and decorations
- ❏ Portable bar
- ❏ Table linens in 21 colors and 10 sizes
- ❏ White lace tablecloth overlays
- ❏ All-white china, plain or with black and gold or silver rims
- ❏ Silver and stainless flatware, 9-piece place settings
- ❏ Square, round, rectangular silver trays
- ❏ Cut glass dishes and punch bowl
- ❏ Every size drinking glass, to include Irish coffee mug
- ❏ Chafing dishes in silver and stainless
- ❏ Serpentine tables to form an oversized circle
- ❏ White laquered folding chairs with padded seats

- ❏ Gold ballroom chairs
- ❏ 36" round rolling table
- ❏ Festive yellow, white, and pink balloon lights
- ❏ Silver coffee and tea service
- ❏ 3-branch silver candelabra
- ❏ 90-cup silver samovar
- ❏ Oak parquet dance floors
- ❏ Striped tents and canopies, creating various sizes and shapes from a 9'x10' entrance canopy to a 40'x80' tent with 3 poles
- ❏ For weddings—flower columns, kneeling bench, wedding arch
- ❏ Champagne fountain (7 gallons)
- ❏ Hot dog roaster
- ❏ Large popcorn machine
- ❏ Convection oven and field oven
- ❏ Garment rack with hangers

Your Special Rental Needs

_____

_____

_____

_____

_____

Restaurant Supply Companies

An alternative to renting party staples—wine glasses, bar glasses, buffet plates, chairs—is stocking your own pantry. This, of course, presumes you have the storage space. Most restaurant supply companies will sell to the public, but they generally do not promote this fact. Their stock-in-trade is durable, moderately priced china and glassware manufactured for commercial use (restaurants, hospitals, cafeterias).

Some TIPS:

♦ A wide range of manufacturers are usually represented (from Libbey Glass to Lenox China) in a myriad of styles and sizes.

♦ Pricing will vary from 30-50 percent off "list" or suggested retail price.

♦ All glass and china are sold in carton quantities. The retail lines are packed in smaller quantities (i.e., 12 pieces to a carton); the commercial-type lines are packed in larger numbers.

♦ Restaurant supply companies also carry a cross section of entertaining staples, from Chinese rice bowls to Japanese teacups, including copper cookware, large volume coffee urns, serving carts, over-sized salad bowls, wine caddies, stainless steel and silver-plated flatware, full place settings, hostess sets, accessory items in china and crockery.

♦ Restaurant suppliers are a good source for different sizes and shapes of folding tables and chairs.

S H O R T   S U B J E C T

What you won't find here is a retail climate. They are wholesalers with no time for retail "niceties," be it chit chat or a return/refund policy. Pre-shop a department store first and take notes. Then browse unobtrusively, order what you need — and beat a fast retreat.

Caterers are the new "Mom" of the 90's. No longer called upon *just* for that grand or elaborate event, these party pros have spread their wings. Their service is an opportunity for all of us whose schedules seldom permit cooking . . . but who are unwilling to trade off the pleasures of entertaining.

THE *ABC'S* OF CATERING

About Caterers

There are two general categories of caterers.

CATEGORY 1: The small one-person operation that will limit itself to food preparation *only*, leaving the issue of outside service staff to the hostess.

CATEGORY 2: The larger catering firm which supplies a cook, necessary staff, food, wine, liquor and will coordinate any party rentals.

A wealth of options permits the large or small, formal or casual party giver the bonus of flexibility. It is the caterer's charge to match your specific needs with their expertise. Remember—Service is their credo.

☞ *You won't have time to cook that birthday dinner for your mother-in-law, but know she expects the old treasured family recipes?* Many caterers will work with your recipes, then deliver the prepared dishes for you to whisk onto the table, accepting all the accolades.

☞ *Your work schedule doesn't permit even a peek at your kitchen, but you want a good "home-cooked" meal for special friends arriving from out of town?* Some very service-oriented caterers will even slip into your home during the day and leave an entire dinner prepared, complete with heating and serving instructions, to greet you and your friends when you arrive home at night.

☞ *Your husband just won the Nobel Prize and you have to entertain the judges and press—next week?* Call the caterer (category #2), take an aspirin and go to bed.

If you don't have a favorite caterer or one that is appropriate for a specific occasion, word of mouth referrals are your best bet. Ask for references when you interview and follow up with phone calls.

Specifics on Menu and Food

Most caterers will design a tailor-made menu specifically for the party; others will have their own repertoire from which you will be asked to select. For a very special or elaborate occasion, you should request a sample tasting of the suggested menu. Shopping for and purchasing all ingredients is the caterer's responsibility.

For logistical purposes, caterers prefer to prepare the food in their own facilities, then, on the day or night of the party, they need only use your kitchen for (1) final touches (heating, steaming, whipping cream), (2) foods that demand last minute attention (soufflés, anything sautéed) and (3) arranging and garnishing plates and platters.

Pricing Guidelines

The great majority of caterers charge on a per-person basis; some up-and-coming ones, however, will only charge time and food, plus mark-up. This latter option actually allows you more flexibility and is kinder to your budget. So don't assume that caterers are an expensive alternative. You'll often find that you would have spent the same amount of money if you had done the shopping and chopping yourself. (And you won't be exhausted.)

$\mathcal{B}$egin with the Particulars

Caterers and their support staff work by the code that they are an extension of the host and therefore provide a vital service. Skilled at organizing, prioritizing and coordinating, a real pro can work magic. Be sure to establish the kind of rapport necessary in a successful working relationship. The trust and confidence that you place in your caterer will let you relax and enjoy your own party.

The following information highlights any questions and situations that might arise when working with this party ally. Start by discussing:

1. The purpose and type of party (if it is to be a large event, there should be a consultation with all the other professionals in volved—florists, party rental, etc.).

2. When, and where it will be held (the where can raise a number of logistical issues).

3. Your likes and dislikes (you are allergic to shellfish; you would like the dessert styled like "this" picture).

4. A brief note on the guests (a menu should be in character with the invitees; certain religions and nationalities have dietary restrictions).

5. Operational notes (i.e., the buffet serving surface can only accommodate three trays; the oven doesn't cook evenly).

6. Timing (i.e., the arrival of guests will be staggered because of other events— necessitating the need for foods that can hold up to a flexible serving time).

Your Personal Notes for Your Caterer

_____

_____

_____

_____

_____

_____

Clear Signals

Additional points to be discussed in the party planning stage—

Serving Portions

Few things are as ungracious as running out of food or as much fun as eating marvelous leftovers. Tell the caterer what constitutes a "serving portion" to you (this can vary from bird-like nouvelle cuisine to hefty man-size). If food is to be presented in buffet style, where plate portions cannot be strictly monitored, allow for an additional percent of each dish.

Service Staff

Be realistic regarding the number of staff necessary to provide adequate service. Cutting corners on sufficient attendants is a high price to pay for frazzled nerves and inconvenienced guests. Also, make any conditions known (i.e., no smoking).

Attire

The appropriate "dress code" is black skirt or slacks, white shirt with black bowties, which is each staff member's responsibility to supply; any special attire or costume is the host's responsibility to provide, at his expense.

Logistics

Logistics cover all those myriad details that assure the party will "come off," not unlike a general mapping out an invasion.

What time do you want dinner served? Where will the bar be set up? Can the tables be situated to take advantage of the blooming perennial border? Where are the outside electrical outlets?

Be sure to discuss contingency plans and back-ups . . . for temperamental ovens, for power failures, for space restrictions.

Clean Up

The Cardinal Rule !
Be very specific up front to guarantee yourself peace of mind after the party. Cover everything, from written instructions regarding the handling of precious breakables (see page 51) to directions for the disposal of garbage.

On serving attendants and support staff ... Every host needs another set of eyes to help monitor the party and assure the guests' comfort. A service staff's first charge is to reinforce the gracious example that the host has set.

The hallmark of a pro? One who anticipates a guest's need, but does not fraternize, talk to or stare at; one who is unobtrusive, but diplomatic, as for example, in gently "steering" guests toward the dining room; one who has a pleasant, neat appearance and countenance and a cheerful willingness to serve.

And now ... the contract, please

At the signing of the contract, a caterer will usually request a deposit (to cover food costs); the balance is to be paid at the end of the party. Determine if payments are to be by cash or check.

Some Key Points:
The contract

The contract should include an itemized description of food, serving portions, brand names for liquor (if supplied by caterer), shot size for drinks, disposition of extra liquor and wine bottles.

❏ If the party giver has to cancel at the last minute, he is responsible for food, labor and any miscellaneous expenses incurred up to that point.

❏ If a party is being catered on a per-person basis, the host will be obligated for the final "head count" to be confirmed on a specific date—whether that number of guests actually shows up for the event.

❏ Caterers carry their own product and food liability insurance and workman's compensation.

❏ Specify the minimum number of hours to be worked by staff and the additional charge for any overtime.

❏ Specific fees should be stipulated for service staff, rentals, etc. and clarify whether host or caterer is responsible for payment.

Rented partyware should be rinsed by the caterer and placed in its original box; tables, chairs, etc. should be folded and put in a secure location, safe from the elements. A recount should confirm the rental contract itemization and be noted on that sheet by the staff person in charge.

Tips From the Pros

1. Treat your caterer as a creative team member, not a servant.

2. Determine who among the staff is the major domo at the party and accountable for smooth operations.

3. LISTEN to the caterer — when he tells you how much staff you will need, why your special food request will not work, what time he should arrive to set up.

4. Don't pinch pennies when it comes to having enough staff.

5. Be ready for the caterer. Clear counters, dish-washer, refrigerator. Show him where all necessary supplies are.

6. Have all serving pieces out and labeled — i.e., first course platter, tray for coffee pot.

7. Stay out of the kitchen. The caterer and his staff are a fine-tuned team. Stop by for one quick "if you need anything, I'll be in the ——" and LEAVE.

The Indispensable Bartender

A "jolly good fellow" is he . . . and the first one you run to call when the thought of a party crosses your mind!
What are the two things that make him indispensable?

❑ His *visibility:* He's the only other person, beside the host, to help insure a good "first impression" on arriving guests.
❑ His *versatility:* which can range from mixing the drinks to helping serve the plates during dinner to cleaning up after the party. (Particulars, should, of course, be dis-cussed and agreed upon in advance.)

To help a bartender carry out his duties effectively, a hostess should:

- o   always express her preferences
- o   provide information about the party, i.e.
       the majority of guests will arrive about _____,
       dinner will be served at _____,
       the jigger strength should be _____,
       plan to close the bar at _____.

Further notes to define and distinguish the indispensable bartender:

♦   He acts as a host's "man Friday," bringing ice, mixes, beverages — and running out to pick up whatever, whenever you, oops, fall short.

♦   He remembers guests' last names and what they first ordered.

♦   He straightens up during and after the cocktail hour, then leaves the kitchen in spic-n-span shape.

♦   His manners are above reproach, characterized by an instinct for timing and judgment.

♦   He is alert to sensitive situations, advising a host, for example, if a guest has over-indulged.

♦   He paces drinks as the party nears dinner time, and departure time.

♦   He helps the hostess with miscellaneous tasks — lighting candles, answering the door, directing guests to dinner.

Party coordinators charge three ways:

▼ a flat fee based on the number of guests;

▼ by the hour; or

▼ by a percentage of cost (approximately 15 percent).

This last option is the least desirable because there is no incentive for keeping costs down.

PARTY PLANNERS
or *Part Me Not From My Rolodex*

This section is intended to provide you with vital information that you may need for that once-in-a lifetime special event. Party planners offer you a welcome alternative in a situation that will be more costly than other entertaining circumstances you deal with on a more regular basis. It is they to whom you turn if you want to avoid tedious details and organizational demands, which include cutting out the hours that you would otherwise spend dreaming up the theme, designing the invitation, tasting caterer's dishes, comparing floral designs, listening to bands, shopping prices. In short, party planners take the guesswork—and heartburn—out of any event.

Their rolodexes yield up a king's ransom in resources; their network insures them the talent of procuring the best product or service at the best price (clout with their subcontractors comes from a promise of future business). Expect additional separate charges for unusual requests or coups — a celebrity that happens to "drop by,"your name up in lights on Times Square, the presence of a live Chinese panda for a children's party.

A written agreement is recommended and some of its points should include:

- ❏ definition of "best price" (no vendor kickbacks or hidden surcharges).
- ❏ specifics outlining exactly what you do want the party planner to do and what you do not want the planner involved in.
- ❏ a checklist to include how and when you want tasks handled.
- ❏ a clause regarding host's approval on all decisions, especially changes.
- ❏ budget, and the procedure should the planner exceed it.

Party planners are indispensable, from arranging to have the pool drained prior to the installation of the dance floor, to paying the wedding bills after the fact. Their responsibilities are limited only by their client's imagination and can include the following:

Designing, printing and mailing invitations

Addressing of invitations and monitoring RSVPs

Developing theme and coordinating decorations, to include flowers, props, handmade table skirts and chair covers

Coordinating production, choreography, set design, lighting (the demand for Broadway-styled production created a sub group of planners now known as "party designers")

Planning menu, hiring caterer and all necessary food service staff

Renting necessary tableware and party furniture, to include tents

Scouting for and renting special locations

Ordering and monitoring all liquor and wine

Arranging for limousines and valet car parks

Selecting entertainment and negotiating these contracts

Hiring video personnel and photographers

Shopping for and buying gifts

Coordinating and shopping for appropriate clothes or costume for host, hostess, staff

Planning events for children to include games, rides, prizes

GREAT ENTERTAINING

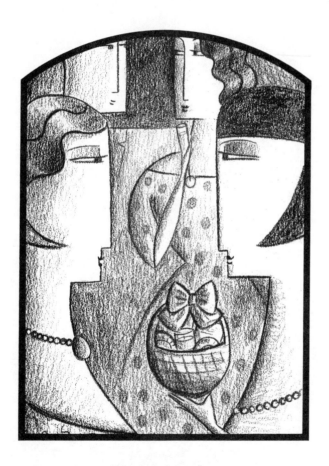

GOOD FORM

GOOD FORM

It's the 1990s. Do you know where your party manners are? Here is a short selection of entertaining happenstance that can be encountered in the life of a party, presented with a bit of tongue-in-cheek.

Ice Breakers
How to get guests to mix and mingle

The following suggestions are meant to inspire the imagination for those situations where party guests may not know each other. Some challenging circumstances may indeed require creative means.

❖ Place a name tag, identifying a famous person, on each guest's back. The guest then has to guess who he is from the questions that other guests ask.

❖ Bring souvenirs from a favorite trip and swap stories.

❖ Start a story and have each guest contribute his own ending, picking up where the previous guest left off.

❖ Before the party, send guests a fictitious humorous book outline for which they must each write a brief, opening introduction; the intros are then read at the party.

❖ Send out a pre-party questionnaire requesting hobbies, favorite places and foods, most harrowing experience, greatest ambition, etc. Then read the answers and have guests guess who it is.

❖ Have a handwriting analyst compare handwritings.

❖ Do the same with a card reader.

Conversation Gambits
Easing In and Out Of Conversations

All too often we are faced with situations that require our attention to be dispersed among a generous number of guests. How should you alight for a few moments, picking up on a conversation already in progress, participate for a few moments, then gracefully move on to another group?

It's a delicate enterprise, requiring subtlety and a good instinct for timing. The subtlety comes in not being so obvious that you break the tempo of the current conversation; the timing comes in knowing when to slip in—and, more importantly, when to ease out.

Understanding a few key points will help you in those occasions when everyone seems to expect "just a moment" with you.

❦ Prepare yourself mentally. Accept the fact that, in this particular social situation, committing yourself quickly in and out of conversations must be your *modus operandi.*

❦ Increase your confidence and comfort level by understanding that if you are *gracious* the conversation will appear *graceful.*

❦ Be sincere and *connect* in those few moments with guests; don't appear distracted or stressed.

❦ Keep your attitude *light.* Avoid weighty topics.

❦ On parting, your concluding words should be particularly supportive and nurturing in tone, to cushion the fact that you aren't engaging in lengthy conversation.

SHORT SUBJECT
How to Get Guests to Mingle

The best icebreaker is still the host—
graciously attentive. . . welcoming you with enthusiasm and making a point of introducing you as though you were the most important person in the room . . . with an enviable memory bank that enables the passing along of little items of interest so that lively conversation begins immediately.

On Easing In

✦   One approach is to hover quietly for a few seconds to pick up on the content of the conversation so that your entry is smooth and not interruptive; it isn't necessary to start talking immediately. But when you do, let it be keyed to their topic. Changing subjects is more tactfully accomplished once you are a group member.

✦   If you want to lead with conversation, avoid introductions. Start instead with a topic, anything in the immediate environment that people can see, smell, hear or touch (dinner aromas, a painting on the wall, the band).

On Easing Out

A new person joining the group provides a distraction and an appropriate opportunity to slip out.

When easing out, use introductions as a vehicle for transferring the attention from your participation to someone or something (the hors d'oeuvres, the city lights).

Let those last few moments and words crystallize your best self—direct eye contact with each person, a posture and tone of voice both upbeat and warm.

A potpourri of one-liners when it's time to move on:

✧   Humorously: "This conversation is getting to heavy for me."

✧   Charm school: "You've obviously got things under control and I'm just going to slip out."

✧   "On that note, I must excuse myself."

✧   "Hold that thought and let's pick it up later."

✧   "Why don't you go over and try the salmon mousse?"

✧   "You all just continue and I'm going to see about John."

✧   "Have you seen the garden in back?"

> **PARDEE TIP**
>
> **A heartfelt compliment is always a good opener, but be careful that it is proferred selectively and at just the right moment.**

The sincerest and most flattering:
"I've really enjoyed this opportunity to chat with you, but if you'll excuse me there are some others that I need to speak to before the party is over."

Conversation Cripplers

We all recognize those traits or practices that jeopardize good conversation— perhaps from being the victim of one or, worse, being guilty of one ourselves. Some are more deadly than others, but to one degree or another the following "Conversation Cripplers" detract from the sheer pleasure that conversation should be:

Half-listening must surely deserve first place as a conversation crippler for the stinging smart that it delivers. Couple it with *Pacificity* and you wonder why you even bothered talking. *Single word answers* and *insincere questions and replies* stifle creativity and make for a dull, tiresome exchange.

Conversation should be cordial, encouraging a give and take which is surely not possible if someone is *talking at or through you*. Nor is it possible if the speaker drones on incessantly, churning out *insincere information* like a computer.

On the other hand, *fabricating* and *overuse of wit* will overwhelm and stifle the listener's attention, while *constant complaining* will chase away the hardiest of souls.

For sheer impact, though, nothing equals the speaker who *monopolizes the conversation*. And these self-centered bores often choose to nourish their sizable egos by *pontificating,* or showing off, ad nauseum.

The final three—*challenging, debating* and *putting down* are not only obstacles to effective conversation, but bring an aggressive and abrasive tone to an otherwise social setting. No discussion of conversation would be complete without a nod to that party character, the bore. While the following ploys are somewhat tongue-in-cheek, we've all probably wished for salvation at one time or another. Hence these **strategies for surviving a bore.**

Strategies
For Surviving A Bore

Some guests are colorful in their affectations. Bores do not know where to draw the line, slipping over the precipice into name dropping, place dropping and money dropping — all the while commencing every sentence in the first person.

And when it's your turn to talk, they suddenly develop a maddening malaise —

the glazed look of disinterest that avoids eye contact; the darting eyes that are constantly seeking a more desirable partner; the inattention that permits constant interruptions at the slightest distraction.

Time to Try:
Party Ploy #1

Stop talking whenever their eyes start to dart. Your choppy, broken sentences should finally catch their attention.

Other prevalent types of bores to be found on the party circuit? Those who:

▼ tell the ending of a book or movie

▼ believe that joke-telling is one of their fortes

▼ trap you in a corner

▼ start a story and then remember, suddenly, that it is not to be told

▼ drink too much

▼ have not refined their smoking habits. Thus they are indifferent to smoke wafting across non-smoker's faces and the appetites of others at the dinner tables as they smoke between courses

▼ insist on telling a story for the nth time, ignoring hints that it has been told before

▼ air family laundry

▼ criticize spouse

▼ become argumentative over the pettiest issue

▼ make unwanted overtures

Experts strongly recommend assertive, not passive tactics when confronted with bores. It takes energy to ignore the "interrupter" and proceed undaunted; wit and liveliness to overwhelm the "dominator" with some of his own patter. *And a non-sensitivity to appearing rude.*

Forewarned is forearmed. Following are some more ploys.

Party Ploy #2.
The butter-wouldn't-melt-in-my-mouth approach—
"You are so fascinating. I must share you with some of the other guests."

Party Ploy #3.
The preemptive move —
"Ah ha, you're the one I've heard so much about. Before we chat, there's someone you simply must meet."

Party Ploy #4.
The best-of-Broadway act—
"Oh, there's ——— trying to get my attention. Let me not be rude to him."

Party Ploy #5.
The cut and run disengagement —
"I'm so sorry. Please do excuse me, but I've got something in my eye/the paté is not agreeing with me/I almost forgot that I was to call ———."

Ah! But what about the situation where mobility has been denied you? As, for instance, at a luncheon table. Should a boring partner not respond to your attempts to establish common grounds for conversation, then try:

Party Ploy #6.
Disarm with a direct and honest approach—
"I'm tired of talking about me. You talk about me."

Party Ploy #7.
Incite with a provocative or debate-inspiring statement—
"If you weren't here, where would you be and what would you be doing?"

Close Encounters
of the Party Kind

Smoking

Host:

Be firm but tactful. *"If you could oblige me,"* or *"With this many guests,"* or *"In such small quarters . . . I would prefer that you not smoke."*

If you are adamant about *absolutely no smoking,* then, you have three choices:
1. Don't invite known smokers.
2. Put a sign on or near your front door, with others scattered through the house. Be prepared to police during the party.
3. Direct smokers outside if they must smoke.

Guest:

Look before lighting up. If no one else is smoking or there are no ashtrays in sight, ask first. If you are asked to smoke outside, remember, it's your obligation as a guest to return to the party. Don't stay outside interminably.

Children

Hostess:

Unless children are well behaved, don't assume guests love having them around. But realize that your interpretation of "well behaved" may not be a guest's.

Guest:

Unless the child or children have specifically been invited, don't assume that they can "tag along." Appreciate the fact that children change the tone of an adult's party, prompting considerations and distractions that a hostess may not have planned on.

SHORT SUBJECT
How to Escape a Bore

Even the most adept partygoers have been known to run out of strategies for dealing with accredited bores. **If all else fails, be ruthless!**

Chin out, take a deep breath, don't drop your guard. And proceed to become a bore yourself.

No matter what their level of experience, children should not sing, dance, recite or otherwise entertain.

If a guest asks to bring a child? Reply, "That just wouldn't be convenient for this particular occasion, but why don't you stop by for a drink?"

UNINVITED GUESTS
Host:

A wise host understands that flexibility goes hand-in-hand with gracious entertaining. But there are times when an unfortunate or sticky situation presents itself. (i.e., the ex-spouse or antagonistic business competitor has been invited.)

If a guest calls because he did not receive an invitation (and you know it was not an oversight):
1. "This is basically a (bridge group, office, literary club, parents of. . .) party, and that's why you didn't receive an invitation." (The "basically" lets you off the hook if the caller finds out later that "others" were included in the party.)
2. "The party had grown so large that we just decided to make it very small this year."
3. "I try to alternate my guest list and since we had you to ———."

If a guest wants to bring a friend:
1. "We're limited space-wise and just must stay with our original guest list."
2. "I've had to turn down other requests and it wouldn't be fair to make an exception."
3. "I've planned this around the special interests of the guests, but I'll quite understand if you feel unable to come without ———."
4. "That just wouldn't be convenient this time, but let's plan on meeting your friend soon."

Guest:

Unless an invitation states, either in formal addressing on the envelope (Ms. Samantha Clayton and Escort/Guest/ Friend) or on the invitation itself, assume that you are invited *alone.* This would be particularly true for a dinner party. If in doubt, call. But unless the hostess enthusiastically accepts your offer to provide another guest at her party, drop the subject to avoid any awkward moments.

ARGUMENTS

Host:

Assuming that a discussion is adding more than the electricity that makes a party stimulating, the tack is the same as with a problem drinker. Be firm.

If humor won't suffice — "What do you think this is, '60 Minutes?'" — exhort the combatants to "get together some place else, at some other time, to finish this discussion PERIOD."

If the argument becomes physical, remove them, or have them removed, as quickly and quietly as possible.

Guest:

If you're responsible for creating an uncomfortable situation for the hostess and/or guests, an apology is due — in writing or by phone.

SHORT SUBJECT
Breakage

Host:

Even if it is your most prized possession, be sensitive to the guest's embarrassment. Don't make a fuss. Clean it up and remove it as quickly as possible.

If attention is called to the mishap, be nonchalant and squelch any discussion of it. Do not let it affect the mood of the party.

Guest:

Offer to help clean up, quickly and unobtrusively.

Apologies should be made quietly, genuinely and briefly. Don't belabor the matter.

If the item was valuable, replace it with its exact or closest counterpart.

Pace yourself by drinking a glass of water between each alcoholic choice. Not only will this help dilute the effects of the alcohol, but it staggers the actual number of cocktails consumed.

DRINKING
Hostess:

With stricter interpretation of the drinking laws, try to head off potential problems by (1) serving enough food, (2) tempering the strength of the drinks, (3) monitoring those over-imbibers.

When problems do occur, take a very straightforward approach — direct the guest to a bedroom for a period of recovery, or overnight, if necessary; call a cab or ask another guest to drive the inebriated home; drive the inebriated guest home yourself.

Be unswerving in your refusal to let an inebriated guest drive, going so far as to escort the individual to the car to make certain that, indeed, someone else will be driving.

Guest:

If you will be driving (1) monitor and pace your consumption, (2) be forthright if you feel even the slightest bit of hesitation regarding your ability to drive responsibly. Yield quietly and graciously to your hostess's or companion's request that someone else drive.

Exit . . . Right

HOST'S GETAWAY:

For those evenings when counting sheep holds more attraction than discussing global problems— start tidying up the room, plumping the cushions, taking stray glasses to the kitchen.

Yawn. Yawn. And yawn some more.

or

Put on your nightshirt and cap and come downstairs with a candle . . . no doubt of your intentions here.

IF ALL ELSE FAILS . . .

Try these quotable quotes for speeding guests on their way:

1. Johnny Carson
   "Would you mind very much dropping the kids off at school on your way home?"
2. Bit of Broadway (hostess to host)
   "Darling, you're keeping everybody up so late."
3. Miss Sympathy
   "You've all been such good sports and I'm not going to keep you up another minute . . . No, no I insist . . . home to bed."
4. Master of the Universe
   "Wow, I had no idea it was so late. We've all got a responsibility to be sharp and alert for our clients.
5. Harriet Hausfrau
   "The dishwasher's broken. Would you mind helping me wash the dishes?"
6. Jet-setter
   "Have you seen our slides of ———? It won't take a second to set up the screen."

SHORT SUBJECT
Guest's Departure

Make it "clean." Avoid dangling farewells that turn into splintered and lengthy conversations, strung out to the street. **Say your good-byes and leave.** The host will love you.

**As host, cue a good friend to start the exodus . . .
with a bit of fanfare if need be.**

7. Bon Vivant (after marshalling the leftovers to the local disco)
   "Gee, I really am tired. Mind if I go home?"
8. Mr. Retiring
   "Stay as late as you like. Just don't forget to turn off the lights, feed the dog and pay the bills."
9. Troop Leader
   "OK, Guys. It's time to wrap this up. All good campers to their tents."

Hostess Gifts

While flowers and wine are the most traditional choices of party guests, these two old standbys pose a dilemma for the host. Consider the typical scenario and it's easy to understand.

Upon being presented with the florist's finest, a hostess is interrupted at that point when she should be giving her full attention to arriving guests and seeing to those very important introductions.

Instead, she must: (1) leave the guests, (2) locate the proper container, (3) cut, prepare and arrange the flowers, (4) decide where they can be shown off to best advantage.

On the other hand, wine provokes a feeling of obligation in the host or implies an expectation on the guest's part regarding the serving of it.

Therefore, the thoughtful guest might consider these alternatives to avoid awkward moments.

SHORT SUBJECT
Gift Suggestions

❦ Bring a small, precious bouquet in its own crystal container or one perfect flower in a special bud vase.

❦ Send flowers after the party, as a pat on the back, or before, with a phone call ahead to determine what selection would complement the hostess's plans.

❦ Give spirits — a favorite bottle of wine, a very old brandy, an exceptional port—with a note that says "just for you . . . to enjoy later."

Many occasions call for commemoration; a new home, remodeled kitchen, upcoming trip. But there is one occasion that all but necessitates an accompanying gift — dining for the first time in someone's home.

The choices for hostess gifts can be as traditional as hand-molded soaps and imported chocolates, or as singular as an embroidered pillowcase or antique desk accessories.

Still perturbed over what to give, if any- thing? Opt for a gift for the children or pet. Doing something for someone's "loved ones" is tantamount to doing it for them.

Other ideas that convey a bit of thoughtful creativity on your part:

▲ hard-to-find and special condiments, herbs, vinegars

▲ scented or beeswax candles

▲ antique tiles to decorate the kitchen or to use as trivets

▲ small fabric or paper covered picture frames

▲ fancy kitchen gadgets

▲ linen hostess towels

▲ unusual bar accessories (a 2 oz. crystal combina- tion pitcher and jigger, or silver lemon peeler)

▲ cotton cocktail napkins in a marvelous Provençal print

▲ a set of pencils covered in Florentine marbled paper

▲ small and unique flower containers

▲ bone-handled canapé or cheese knives

▲ sachets for the closet, scented papers for drawer liners

▲ sterling silver makeup accessories

▲ a phone-side box of note paper

▲ porcelain stamp holder

▲ fabric-lined invitation stand

▲ hand-painted or de- coupaged small baskets

GREAT ENTERTAINING

LIVING FAST/ENTERTAINING WELL

Living Fast/ Entertaining Well

When life seems to be on fast forward . . . some friendly advice and well-researched—and rehearsed—pointers on entertaining in the non-stop '90s.

Five Big Housekeeping Secrets

or How to Find More Time to Entertain

① **Chunk down.**
Follow the old adage:
*Inch by inch it's a cinch
Yard by yard it's hard.*
Chop every big job down into little doable jobs.

② **Schedule your time.**
Develop a 15-20 minute "presentable house" straightening and cleaning schedule that you can live with on a daily basis.

③ **Do away with clutter**
or keep it down considerably by finding, creating or reworking a "place for everything." Sweep clutter aside before starting any clean-up.

④ **Make each step count.**
Pick up and clean as you go. Never make a move empty-handed.

⑤ **Organize better.**
Keep up with new organizational aids on the market; be on the lookout for tips in magazines and newspapers; avail yourself of organizing professionals; ask friends.

Prepping the House

Inside and Out

A 10-Point Checklist to keep your home in party-ready shape.

1. Test smoke and heat detectors 2 - 3 times a year.

2. Keep a fire extinguisher in working order and place in an accessible location.

3. Take care of wiring problems — both the house and appliances. (Don't forget the pool light.)

4. Wax wooden floors properly so they aren't slippery.

5. Put skid-proof padding under all rugs, especially throw rugs.

6. Chemically soil-repel as many upholstered furnishings as possible.

7. Repair or re-grout chipped or broken bricks, tile, stone in walkways, steps and patios.

8. Invest time and money in bug reduction products for summer entertaining.

9. Avoid a smoke-filled room at party time by testing the fireplace if it has not been used for a season or two.

10. Hide house keys in a secure, but convenient location outside.

In the Marketplace ...

Look for —
* The small emergency light that illuminates a room or hallway the instant current fails.

* Solar-powered garden lights that can be staked or wall-mounted; the photocell automatically turns light on at dusk, off at dawn.

Your House Checklist

_____

_____

_____

_____

_____

_____

_____

A utilitarian and attractive answer to the ultimate clutter catcher, a wastebasket?
Use large (approximately 14"-18" high) florist's baskets pre-lined with plastic. Leave in their natural rattan state or spray paint to coordinate with a specific room.

Housekeeping Strategies

▲ Break an organizational rule. Save one catch-all drawer specifically for junk and clutter.

▲ Invest in space-saving equipment — ironing boards that collapse into a drawer or hang from a closet rod; mini under-cabinet appliances.

▲ Do last minute polishing, and keep your hands clean at the same time, using a silversmith's glove.

▲ Use a rubber grid sink mat to protect fine glasses and dishes when hand washing.

▲ Keep all cleaning products in a plastic basket that is transportable to clean-up spots.

▲ Use door mats and small throw rugs to stop the track of dirt from people and animals.

▲ Use self-stick felt strips to protect furniture from rough-bottomed serving dishes, flower containers, decorative objects.

▲ Protect upholstered furniture with contour fitted arm covers; keep them in place with "corkscrew" pins.

▲ Use rolling carts for ease of transporting food, projects, supplies (even clutter) quickly from one area to another.

▲ Rotate area rugs and furniture to offset uneven wear and tear.

▲ Hang up anything that can be wall- or under cabinet-mounted

Quick Decorating Pointers
For *Easy* Party Giving

❖ Comfortable and inviting seating immediately puts guests at ease. Be practical about its arrangement. Seating should be close enough for people to talk without straining, but open enough to allow them to circulate comfortably.

❖ Be sensitive to a party's flow. Eliminate or relocate any furniture that will cause a bottleneck. If using a portable bar, locate it in an area with plenty of space around it. Not only will it be the highest trafficked area of the party, but conversations started at the bar take a while to break up and move on. Use the positioning of the bar as an opportunity to move guests into the party and away from the front door.

❖ Be sure to have a few small "occasional" chairs that can be easily moved by a guest to create their own tête à tête.

❖ Don't forget those handy, small "drink tables."

❖ Ottomans with casters are indispensable for party giving. Push or pull them whenever, or wherever, additional seating is needed. Plus, the wisely designed ottoman will seat two people.

❖ Dispense with spindly-legged chairs and tables that give guests the feeling they are the proverbial bull in a china shop.

NOTE

If a hostess has some treasures that she would be nervous about in the course of a party, she should know exactly how to care for them in the event of a mishap (i.e., red wine spilled on an antique lace tablecloth).

A decorator advises:
After a party is over, look at how guests have pulled up or
re-arranged chairs. This is a good reference point for
improving your room's seating plan.

❖ If buffet dinners are
your style — consider a
coffee table of a size and
height that can be
cleared easily to accom-
modate diners; keep a
good supply of attrac-
tive folding chairs.

❖ For maximum flexibility,
your main lighting in
each room should be
controlled by a dimmer;
be sure to have enough
indirect lighting to help
sustain "atmosphere."

❖ Position your sound
system so that it is easily
accessible.

❖ Design and organize
your bar so that it is func-
tional enough for guests
to use by themselves.

❖ Keep a few low-
maintenance green
plants in your main

entertaining areas. Then
temporary flower ar-
rangements need only
enhance this permanent
greenery.

❖ Keep a mental record of
a few favorite flower
vases and their strategic
spots in each room.
This will save you time
at the florist when pre-
paring for a spur-of-the-
moment gathering.

❖ If you're shopping for
more table space, con-
sider a table with fold-
down leaves that can be
folded out, pre-party, to
hold cheese trays, hors
d'oeuvres platters, etc.

Entertaining in Small Spaces

Urban living, and its attendant apartment dwelling, can be a mixed blessing. Nowhere is that truer than the trade-offs that must be made when entertaining—no grassy lawn for the children and dogs to frolic on, no brick terrace where Dad can set up the barbecue, no spacious dining room or kitchen for a host of friends to sit and chat.

Ah, yes. With apartment living comes the necessity to "think small." Time to acquaint yourself with . . .

"STANDARD OPERATING PROCEDURES". . .

For people with big ideas and little space

▼ Organize dedicated space to high-priority daily activities so that constant clearing away isn't necessary when you want to entertain.

▼ Have entertaining staples together in one easily accessible storage spot.

▼ Look for ways to create temporary storage space during party time. On a volume basis, a bathtub or shower stall is a potent storage weapon — for everything from a make shift guest coat rack to stackable clutter and furniture that can be hidden behind a shower curtain.

POST IT

"Square footage" becomes part of your vocabulary when living in restricted spaces. Translated for party purposes, that means 5 square feet of floor space per person.

Hang up anything that can be wall- or under-cabinet mounted.

Time Out for Some Words About *Clutter Catchers*

These suggestions for inevitable emergency party tidy-ups should be saved specifically for this purpose. Peace of mind comes with knowing that you have one or two dedicated places for quickly dispensing with clutter.

- long shelves that are placed high, near the ceiling, up and out of the way

- a hinged living room trunk styled as an ottoman seat

- a single drawer in a piece of furniture that is conveniently located

- baskets that are hung from a kitchen ceiling or pan rack

- an under-bed storage drawer

- an out-of-use fireplace with decoratively painted wooden screen

Two Facts of Life for Small Spaces

1. Rooms should be adaptable. A room is only a setting for people and their lifestyle, so don't be locked into single-purpose definitions. Press any room into service. A dining space can be created in a library, cocktails can be served in a dressing room, a buffet can be set up in a hallway. Yes, if a bathroom has more than its fair share of space, figure it into your party logistics, too.

Take Note: Partying in unorthodox places contributes its own sense of fun.

Small spaces act as great icebreakers because no one can hide in a corner.

**Casters on furniture will ease the transformation
process when rearranging for parties.**

2. Furniture should be multi-functional. This means:
    o adaptable to any entertaining purpose
    o movable
    o collapsible, foldable
       or stackable

What furniture makes the best use of space?

*Keep these points in mind when making decorating purchases.
Your furnishings have to pull their own weight.*

+ L-shaped sofa

+ Movable unit seating

+ Seating at right angles

+ Two small coffee tables
  that can be separated

+ Nesting tables

+ Table with one or two
  leaves, that can be
  placed against the wall,
  pulled out for dining

+ Pedestal table that is
  coffee table height in one
  position, dining height
  in another

+ Coffee table with pull-
  out ottomans under-
  neath

+ Any small piece of furniture that can support a
  larger, folding circular
  table top for dining

+ A tea cart that can move
  an entire dinner from
  kitchen to dining room,
  be set up as a buffet in
  any room, move clutter
  in pre-party organizing

+ The classic hardwood
  "butler's buffet," with
  brass hinges and a
  galleried edge that flips
  down to create a gener-
  ous 35-inch surface.
  With casters and a lower
  shelf, it's great as a portable bar or TV/stereo
  stand, when not in use
  as an extra serving table.

Glass kitchen cabinet doors give a feeling of greater space.

What about the Kitchen?

◇ Organize for your entertaining style. Do you prefer to:
Cook ahead or count on frozen foods?
You'll need a larger fridge, more freezer and food storage facilities
or
Prepare fresh on the spot?
You'll want the maximum amount of working space and room for equipment.

◇ Create as much unbroken counter surface as space will permit. This is more convenient and flexible than 2 or 3 smaller, separate sections.

◇ Buy the best — the more restricted the space, the more wear and tear on equipment, floors, appliances.

◇ For maximum efficiency: Store every item closest to where it is most often used. Store everyday items between shoulder and hip height so there is no bending and stretching. Install a flip-up table on the back of a door for entertaining clean-up demands. Invest in under-the-cabinet mounted appliances

◇ Make use of every inch. For a kitchen buffet, fill the sink with ice to hold a salad bowl or other cold dish; or cover with cutting board to create another serving surface.

Hostess on the Go

OK, So you didn't follow the instructions on page —, you lost the party planner's checklist and the living room hasn't been vacuumed in three weeks.

And, you only have 15 minutes before the thundering herds descend upon you.

Here's *how to-look-like-you-weren't-caught-off-guard-when-you've-really-done-next-to-nothing.*

❦ **Go for show.**
Attention to details will make it look like you've *thought* of (and therefore *done*) everything.

❦ **Don't sweat the small stuff.**
Like cleaning.
Even experts have trouble ascertaining when a rug has been vacuumed. This is where your trusty cordless vacuum comes in for special pick ups.

❦ **Play up mood enhancers.**
A lot can be overlooked when guests feel pampered and at ease in a warm, gracious atmosphere. It's as easy as
1. *music*
2. *flowers*
3. *candles*

This list is ranked in order of priorities.
Start your countdown!

1. Music on.
   You deserve some background accompaniment.

2. Flowers out.
   Spot single bud vases around the room, including the guest bathroom.

3. Candles lit.

4. Freshen the room with potpourri, room spray or fragrant votives.

5. Straighten or put away clutter.
   Straightening is faster and most people won't presume that *anything* is clutter if it's in neat stacks or row.s

6. Fluff cushions and pillows.

7. Put out fresh towels in the guest bath.

8. Clean sink and polish chrome in bathroom.

9. Put out a new bar of soap.

10. Put out a new roll of toilet paper

11. Empty wastebaskets.

12. Set the table.

13. Lower the lights:
    This makes everything seem calmer, even if you're not. This also cloaks any dusting that you didn't have a chance to do.

14. Close off those rooms you did not get to.

15. Spritz your face with mineral water for a quick pick-up.

Your Countdown Checklist

1. _____
2. _____
3. _____
4. _____
5. _____
6. _____
7. _____
8. _____
9. _____
10. _____
11. _____
12. _____
13. _____
14. _____
15. _____

Crises I Have Known

or What Mother Forgot to Tell Me About Entertaining

Heed these lessons. They are an attempt to spare you from encountering, or at least, repeating the following gems. (The fact that each of these scenarios has happened to me at one point or another is purely coincidental.)

SCENE #1:
Pre-party dialogue regarding new kitten.

BBP: "I don't know if we should leave him out. He's a little squirrelly around strangers."

JHP: "Well, we can't lock him in the closet. He'll be OK."

Party Time:
Older guest sitting in over-stuffed living room chair. Kitten, patrolling on mantle, executes a flying dismount, landing on top of chair. Then proceeds to slide into guest's bouffant hairdo.

LESSON #1:
Do **NOT** assume guests will love your furry little darling as much as you do. In fact, don't even assume they like animals.

It is the total converse of a gracious welcome to have an arriving guest greeted by a barking, jumping dog. Or a well-intended friend receiving a nip as thanks for his patting and petting. Not to mention the issue of allergies.

In short, your pet's good manners are important, too. If they're questionable, then *your* good manners must intercede.

"If I know I've done everything to insure a good party, I just go on and have fun, come what may."

SCENE #2:
Pre-party cleaning and decorating.

BBP: "Did you remember to move the two big Ficus trees in from the sun porch? How are we going to get by with out those chairs that are still at the upholsterer's? Do you think it's OK to leave the magazines in the bathroom? Should we use silver trays or rattan baskets?"

JHP: "What are you making such a big deal about? We're not having Prince Charles and Diana for a house tour."

LESSON #2:

Entertaining is a pleasure too good to miss because the house isn't magazine picture perfect.

Our home is the most personal of statements, representing all manner of taste levels and idiosyncrasies. No wonder there is a bit of anxiety surrounding its exposure to others.

Should we try to have a party before the shutters are painted "*House Beautiful*-approved" green? Will they think Chinese red walls are too wild? Does the house look too contemporary, too eclectic, too traditional? Will they notice that there's no furniture against that wall?

Yes and No.

Now, remember back to parties that were really **FUN.** You'll be reminded of a great truth. *Good* parties have nothing to do with the color of the walls or whether the sofa pillows were pure silk. Once up and going, a memorable time depends on intangibles—the gracious spirit of the host, the atmosphere of conviviality, the synergism of the guests. *Not* on tangible objects.

Scene #3:

BBP in tub. JHP, sweaty, just coming in from mowing the lawn. Doorbell rings. First guest arrives.

BBP: "They're not supposed to be here for 45 minutes. What time *is* it?

JHP: "The bedroom clock says 6:15 pm. but my watch says 7:00 pm. Oh, no! I forgot the fuses blew when I was putting in the window air conditioner."

Lesson #3:

Remember Murphy's Law? If something can go wrong, it will. So keep a sense of humor at the ready and be prepared to do some quick thinking. You're just as human as your guests. Handling a mini-crisis with wit and aplomb will endear you to them.

Some hosts (and more often than not, guests) even secretly relish the unexpected for the spark of adventure that it injects.

Scene #4:

Dinner time.
Stuffy boss and wife in living room. New associate and frazzled wife in kitchen, with meal in mixed state of readiness.

BBP: "I *told* you the upper oven was broken and to turn on the lower one."

JHP: "These quail will take at least an hour to cook. And what about that frozen daiquiri soufflé? Why couldn't we just do something simple? The boss's stomach has been growling for an hour.

Lesson #4:

Don't bite off more than you can chew. Before embarking upon a specific event, calmly evaluate all factors — your strengths, your weaknesses, the necessary logistics, special considerations, i.e., your galley-sized kitchen has a temperamental oven; you never quite mastered those French soufflés in the one cooking course you took; the new project at the office doesn't leave you with much time flexibility.

Factor in all these givens and tailor a gathering that suits *your* circumstances at a specific point in time.

SCENE #5:
Room full of guests. Bar set up in antique cupboard, with glass protecting the counter surfaces.

JHP: "Help yourself to the bar while I check the oven."

GUEST: "Do you want me to use this pitcher for the water?" Cracked pitcher handle snaps. Pitcher lands on glass top and both shatter.

LESSON #5:
It's not what happens to you, it's how you handle it. Living by this credo takes the starch out of those inevitable incidents. Four quick steps will see you through this scenario:

❖ Make certain no one is hurt.
❖ Wave off any concern.
❖ Go on cheerfully like nothing had happened.
❖ See to the mishap quickly and quietly.

A cool head will sharpen your wits and judgment, whereas collapsing into a state of agitation will only make others uncomfortable—not to mention the dampening effect it has on the party.

SCENE #6:
An evening in the life of Ms. Partygiver.
Guests due at 6:30
BBP arrives home at 5:30
The following has to be accomplished in one hour:

PARDEE TIP

Some old, but reliable advice
Keep crises in perspective by asking yourself how you'll feel about it a year from now.

Unpack case of wine and chill three bottles.
Feed cat.
Straighten up living room and dining room.
Clean bar and buffet table glass.
Set up the bar.
Set the table.
Arrange centerpiece.
Polish candlesticks.
Fix hors d'oeuvres plate.
Decide on serving pieces and utensils.
Wash, stuff chicken.
Cut snow peas and red peppers.
Wash and cut four lettuces.
Make lemon-butter sauce.
Cut scallions.
Cut walnuts.
Mix salad dressing.
Wash rice, cook rice.
Dress.
Actual elapsed time: 2 hours and 4 minutes

JHP: "Why don't you ever give yourself enough time?"

BBP: *silence*

LESSON #6:

Don't put off the inevitable, hoping that your knack for survival will see you through.

Old Time does have a way of slipping by . . . faster, it seems, if you haven't budgeted the proper amount in the first place. Be cold-blooded in your evaluation of how much time preparations will take — from planning to shopping to chopping. Then factor in an additional 20 percent for a cushion. And then factor in yet another 20 percent for time thieves like walking time, driving and parking time, phone interruptions, children's emergencies, switching over to a contingency plan. In short, party preparations will probably take about 50 percent more time than you had originally calculated.

Taming
the Perfection Complex

We've been there before, with the butterflies in the stomach, the certainty that something was going to go wrong, the apprehension over how the meal would taste. To some, just being able to begin the process of party giving is insurmountable.

I call it the "Perfection Complex" and it can be crippling. You're afraid if the meal doesn't qualify as "gourmet," the table setting isn't "elaborate" and the local paper won't describe it as the "ultimate," that it isn't worth attempting at all. Best to wait, you say, 'til some other time when everything can be perfect.

Now, remember back to those parties where you really had a *good* time, where you felt completely at ease, where you were experiencing that "warm tummy" feeling that comes from satisfying, unfussy food? Where the genuine friends made you feel good about yourself and still others were so fascinating that you felt you could talk for hours? Where you swore you'd never laughed so hard in your life?

All of those impressions had nothing to do with the perfection of decor or meal. What counted was the spirit of good-natured congeniality, the relaxed and fun attitude, where cares and concerns were put on hold.

Revive those memories when you start to put off a party because . . .

Each time you entertain it becomes easier. You find your own comfort level. Your confidence is reinforced. Your expectations become less unrealistic. And then you learn how to manage that old unmanageable—an obsession with perfection.

Eau de Stress

Use that pre-party adrenaline surge as your ally to sharpen your creativity, fine-tune your wits, give an edge to your attentiveness. Coping with other forms of stress, or distress, however, deserves some practical tips.

❦ *Think Positive.* Concentrating on your vision of the ideal party situation or outcome reduces anxious anticipations. Even if something doesn't go according to plan, at least you have not burdenedyourself with before-the-fact worries. Take comfort — many hostesses believe something going awry adds zest to a party.

❦ *Stay Loose.* See the pluses in going with the flow and reassessing and reevaluating. Practice making "lemonade out of lemons."

❦ *Accept the total package* that is YOU. Live by describing yourself as the host you seem to be rather than evaluating yourself as what you should be.

❦ *Act, don't react.* Anticipate situations that "hit a nerve" and learn to manage your response. Pay attention to, and try to reduce those factors that make entertaining challenging for you.

❦ *Set realistic goals.* Underschedule and underdemand yourself so that you can underwhelm yourself.

❦ *Become your own best friend.* Learn to say **no** while learning to give yourself permission to take care of yourself (see Beauty Tips).

❦ *Laughter* is the ultimate stress manager. Know what, or who, "tickles your fancy" and schedule it into your day — and parties!

Looking Out for Number 1

Great party givers give top priority to taking care of themselves. For a host or hostess to feel less than great about themselves is an unnecessary distraction. If you haven't already done so, proceed with firm conviction to integrate the following into your lifestyle:

Be Good to Yourself

ॐ Don't plan a party if it's going to be a hectic week, or an otherwise emotionally trying time.

ॐ Develop the art of mental visualization. Gather your thoughts and go through a creative "dress rehearsal." Picture every detail of your party from start to successful completion.

ॐ On the day of the party, indulge in a relaxing ritual, a restorative that you save just for this occasion. It can be as simple as a nap or bubble bath, but its importance is that *it's a present you give yourself.*

ॐ If need be, during the party, take short (5 minute) breaks to catch your breath, collect your thoughts.

ॐ Drink a warm glass of milk, or take calcium supplements, to relax and ensure a good night's sleep before the party.

ॐ Pamper *yourself* with details. Use that fine china teacup and special scented soap (don't "save" them just for guests); keep your favorite fresh flowers around every day (even a single bud vase is sufficient).

Stay Well-informed

Learn to tell amusing stories, to be a sympathetic and good listener, to mix a Manhattan or a Caesar salad without a fanfare. Know the difference between a Browning Sonnet and a Browning over and under, between Beethoven, Brancusi and the Baltimore Orioles . . . and to enjoy poking fun at yourself.

The luxury of leisure comes with careful planning.
Promise yourself that you'll be finished with preparations
and relaxing in the bath one hour before guests arrive.

Develop a Fitness Regimen

This is an absolute requisite for being energetic and in
control. Through regular exercise we:

◇ direct "nervous" energy.
◇ provide a healthy distraction.
◇ make good use of extra adrenaline.
◇ relax our bodies.

Don't forget to include relaxation and meditation in this
category.

Quick Pre-Party Pick-ups

♦ Mist a tissue with min-
eral water, lay it on your
face for 30 seconds and
peel it away. Surface
dirt and oil will bond
with the water and come
right off. Then, dust
with translucent powder
for a quick polish.

♦ Brighten up instantly
with a quick coat of
lipstick and blush.

♦ Use soft, pliable plastic
eye packs, kept cold in
the fridge, for a soothing
refresher.

♦ Take a whirlpool bath.
Check out the safe, self-
contained, portable
versions that convert
your plain tub instantly
to a relaxing personal
spa.

♦ Lie on your bed or floor,
with feet at a 45-degree
angle to the wall. Blood
rushing to the head is a
quick reviver; legs bene-
fit too.

Dressing Do's and Dont's

Dressing Do's

▲ Do clip up a notepad in your closet for listing alterations, shoe repairs as they occur. Then address on a regular basis. This lets you avoid disappointment and frustration the night of your party (or anyone else's) when you discover the too-long hem or torn cuff.

▲ Do consider the ironing board that mounts within a drawer and telescopes out for use; folds down and away when drawer is closed. With this convenient product, you'll be more inclined to iron the evening's dress or freshen up dinner napkins.

▲ Do decide what you are going to wear a few days ahead.

▲ Do dress in something that lets you be "the hostess you've always wanted to be." But don't be so creative that guests feel over- or under-dressed.

Dressing Don'ts

If you're going to be in the kitchen a lot:

▼ Don't wear "hot" fabrics (polyester or wool).

▼ Don't wear anything with blouson sleeves that can go up in flames or drape through the gravy.

▼ Avoid makeup that will suffer from the heat.

▼ Don't choose tight or constricting clothes that restrict your flexibility and ease of movement.

▼ Skip metallic jewelry—it can heat up very quickly when you're working around the oven.

Keep a mirror in the kitchen, with one lipstick, for quick touch-ups. This saves a separate trip to the bedroom or bath.

Beauty and Dressing Tips Time-savers

1. Invest in one of the latest cordless mini-hair appliances. All are scaled down for flexibility and travel-ability so that you can revive your tresses at the office, in the air, on the road.

2. Make your next hair-cutting, coloring, etc. appointment as you are paying your bill for the present visit. It eliminates one more "to do" on your list.

3. Know when your hair looks its best — the day you leave the salon or 2 weeks later when the cut, color or perm has leveled out— and coordinate this with your party date.

Your Personal Beauty and Dressing List

_____

_____

_____

_____

_____

_____

_____

_____

_____

_____

_____

_____

_____

_____

GREAT
ENTERTAINING

ENTERTAINING ESSENTIALS

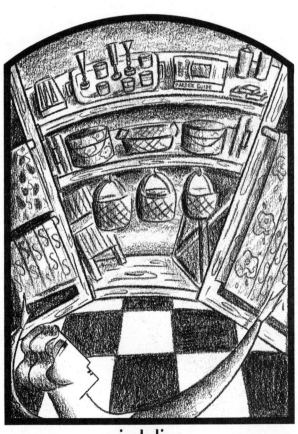

including
Party Planner's Guidebook

Entertaining Essentials

Storage and Organization Strategies

There can be no great entertaining without some great organizing. And some of that organizing has to take place far behind-the-scenes . . . in closets, pantries and storage rooms.

"Your mission, should you decide to accept" . . . is to create an organized storage area for all your entertaining needs. Where do you begin?

1. Give careful thought to your style of entertaining. Do you prefer casual Sunday kitchen suppers to more formal seated Saturday night buffets?

2. List all the party staples, supplies and accessories that this type of entertaining requires; measure large or over-sized pieces (trays, chairs, tabletops).

3. Locate one place in your home — preferably a pantry, but hopefully at least a nook or cranny — and design it to accommodate as many of your entertaining staples as space will permit.

4. Avail yourself of all the organizational aids available in stores and catalogs, from modular shelf systems to custom drawer dividers.

5. Repeat in your sleep — *"Accessibility is one of the keys to successful and easy entertaining."*

> **Protect your silver accessories and reduce polishing needs at the same time.** Tarnish-resistant silversmith cloths come in a wide assortment of bags, rolls, zippered pouches. They are also available by the yard to line drawers, shelves, inside of cabinets.

A Party Giver's *Ideal* Pantry

- candlesticks; plus bo-beches, felt candle pads, candle sharpener

- tapered candles (keep partial supply in freezer)

- votive holders plus any decorations (i.e., gold leaves to wrap around at holiday time)

- votive candles, sterno, denatured alcohol

- place cards, menu cards, Party Planner's Guide-book, movable seating chart

- tablecloths and table squares (Hang on sturdy wooden hangers or across deep towel bars.)

- place mats and napkins (store flat in drawer, in linen press, in file folders by set, or hang from wire hanger with clothespin)

- napkin rings and napkin holders

- baskets

- potpourri, room freshener spray

- silvercloth-lined slots for vertical storage of silver trays and platters

- silvercloth-lined divided drawer, or portable zippered version, for silver place settings and flatware

- silvercloth-lined cabinets for all other silver

- rolling cart

- folding chairs, plus slipcovers

- folding tables in assorted sizes, plus felt "silence cloths"

- felt-covered folding table tops

- collapsible commercial coat rack (also indispensable when packing for a long trip)

PLUS: all china, crystal and silver and accompanying serving pieces

Organize Your Pantry

No "ideal pantry?"
Consider these creative alternatives for smarter storing.

In Closets:
The key is to consider space from a volume standpoint, not just length and width; figure height into the equation, also,

1. Rework with do-it-yourself plastic-coated wire shelving modules. There are endless combinations, including baskets and sliding drawers.

2. Take advantage of "hanging organizers" if you don't want to rework an entire closet. Soft-sided cloth storage accessories, including shelves, can be adapted to entertaining needs.

3. Fill open shelves with bright paper-covered hat boxes, floral fabric organizer-modules, vinyl storage chests.

Create storage space from "dead areas":

◇ over the bathtub, under stairs, end of a hall

◇ out of the way or informal area walls where pegboard facilitates hanging shelves, odds and ends

Let spaces serve double-duty:

♦ Hang inside-back of closet doors with shallow wire shelves.

♦ Alternate painted wicker storage baskets along a hallway, up a stairway.

♦ Design your own pantry, of any size, on any available wall with easily-assembled wooden modular shelf systems.

♦ When doing any storage planning, think ahead to what you will be adding or acquiring in the future.

♦ Elegantly designed "library books" are a secret cache for all your CD's, tapes, video cassettes, party organizing file.

♦ Adapt one of the kitchen-center-on-wheels as your "mobile" pantry.

♦ Organize your kitchen by party style: dishes for large parties (roasters, casseroles, serving trays) in one place; hors d'oeuvres platters and bowls for cocktail parties in another area.

Party Planner's Guidebook

*On the following pages are the
necessities for any entertaining effort,
distilled down into "user friendly" checklists,
references, planners and monitors*

Take in hand and use right now

OR

Tailor to your own specific needs

Entertaining Journal

Occasion **Bands in town for wedding** Style/Theme **High Tea**
Date **Sun., Dec. 5** Time **6:00-9:00** Location **pool house tent**
Attire **Edwardian** Invitations mailed **Nov. 20th**

Original Guest List (*attendees)

* Kathy & Pete Hendrick
* Frank & Vanya Rohner
  Patsy & Charlie Cappel
* Marie Vacarelli
  Dan Schmidt
* Nancy & Henry de Nero

* Sara Bearden & Bill Boynton
* Ruthie & Jimmy Watts
* Ginny & Guy Millner
* Cheri & John Langhorn
* Hoot McCullough
  Pam & Bob Connell

Menu	Details
Neopolitan Sandwiches	My Dress: **claret velvet w/ gold pleated jacket**
Assorted cheese & crackers	
Cold leg of lamb w/ "Charleston" rolls	Flowers (table): **Amaryllis, baby eggplant, ivy, berries**
Meat Pies · egg & caviar roulade	Other:
Holiday Fruit Bread	Decorations: **claret moiré table cloths w/ gold net oversquares**
Marble cake · Cider cake	Music: **Harp**
Mincemeat tarts	
Frozen Hazelnut Souffle	Entertainment:

Service/Rentals	Fee Paid	Notes
Photographer **Bernard Cohen**	200.	• well-rec'd alternative to cocktail party
Bartender **Ross** @20./hr.	180.	
Caterer **Jane Ferguson**	178.	• Sue passed along idea for mother-daughter tea
Server(s) **Charles J., Wilford @ 15.**	90.	
Rentals		• Consider sherry & champagne instead of drinks
15 gold ballroom chairs 3 small café tables Tent		• Wilford for bartender

Entertaining Journal

Occasion _____ Style/Theme _____

Date _____ Time _____ Location _____

Attire _____ Invitations mailed _____

Original Guest List (*attendees)

_____   _____
_____   _____
_____   _____
_____   _____
_____   _____
_____   _____

Menu	Details
	My Dress:
	Flowers (table):
	Other:
	Decorations:
	Music:
	Entertainment:

Service/Rentals	Fee Paid	Notes
Photographer		
Bartender		
Caterer		
Server(s)		
Rentals		

Party Resources Rolodex

To include:
Contact name, address, phone number, (special emergency numbers if available), business hours, location notes. (Assumes that fire, hospital, ambulance, babysitter are in separate location.)

EXAMPLE

FLORIST, WINSTON'S
Audrey   848-5880

3320 Boylston St.   02116

9:00-6:00
Park in lot behind drugstore on corner

A sampling of some party resources:

Party Planner
Bartender
Grocer
Florist
Caterer
Servers
Party Rental
Restaurant
Supply
Hairdresser
Seamstress
Kennel
Liquor Store
Ice Store
Cab
Limousine
Valet Parkers
Hardware Store
Calligrapher
Post Office
Copy Center

Xerox
Part-Time Secretarial
Answering Service
Emergency Electri-
    cian Emergency
Plumber
24 Hr. Pharmacy
Maid Services
Garbage Pickup
Window Washers
Floor Polishers
Rug Cleaners
Tent Rental
General House
    Cleaning Services
Chimney Sweep
Upholstery Cleaners
Engraver
Record and Stereo
    Store

Costume Rental
Uniform and Tuxedo
    Rental
Veterinarian
Bakery
Fish Market
Meat Market
Floral Designer
Pool Service
Yard Service
Courier
Party Designers
Wrapping and Ship-
    ping Service
Musicians
Lighting Expert
Sound System
    Resource
Security Officers
Rent-A-Mom

MENU—*Food and Equipment Shopping List*

Here, in one quick glance, you have not only your party menu, but preparation notes, the individual pieces in which each dish will be served, and a grocery list.

Under *serving piece*, note the individual item in which each dish will be served. Also note any miscellaneous details (i.e., handle needs repair).

In the *menu* column, record the specific dish, recipe, source with page number, recipe serving quantity, approximate preparation time, cooking time and oven temperature.

The *shopping list* column gives you the advantage of noting all ingredients and needs at the same time that you are making up the menu. Equipment needs and purchases should be listed also.

CODE:	* Prepare ahead
	+ Equipment purchase

Serving Piece	Menu	Shopping List
Antique silver basket	**Puff pastry cheese straws** HB 11/88 p. 132 (serves 32) Prep time: 40 mins. Cook: 18 mins. Oven: 400 degrees F.	2 10"x10" frozen puff pastry 2/3 cup fresh parmesan paprika; cayenne; eggs whole milk carrots celery
(Kitchen)	**Gingered Carrot Soup w/ toasted whole grain bread** garnish: creme fraiche (8) Vogue Ent. Winter '88 p. 130 Prep time: 35 mins. Cook: 20 mins.	fresh ginger thin whole grain bread cream 5 lemons lamb fresh rosemary mint jelly *bread crumbs hazlenuts
Large oval silver platter (Aunt Jane)	**Roast Saddle of Lamb** w/ hazlenut & rosemary crust (8) Met. Homes Spring '86 p. 102 Prep time: 15 mins. Cook: 2 1/4 hrs. Oven: 350 degrees F.	fennel bulbs small white turnips small parsnips baby leeks haricots vert baby artichokes baby eggplants baby onions with greens baby yellow acorn
above	**Glazed baby vegetables** (8) Met. Home Spring 86 p. 101 Prep time: 50 mins. Code: 10-12 mins.	squash

Serving Piece	Menu	Shopping List
Small round silver tray w/ fluted edges	**Madeleines** (12) NYT p. 91 Prep. time: 20 mins. Cook: 25 mins. Oven: 350 degrees F.	zucchini (2c. shredded) 1/2 cup parmesan buttermilk baking mix + madeleine pan cream of tartar butter + 10" tart shell flour lemon leaves
round, footed silver tray	**Lemon Soufflé Tart** (8) NY 10/24/88 p. 83 Prep. time: 35 mins. Cook: 18 mins. Oven: 400 degrees F. (make tart shell: 20 mins.)	

TAKE-AWAY RESOURCES—*Menu*

Develop a resource list of take-out food stores, within
____x____ miles of your home. Include hours, location,
delivery notes. Obtain menus and food listings whenever
possible. Then plan a few party menus of your own based
on what's available and keep it handy for spur-of-the-
moment entertaining.

Menu	Source	Hours	Phone	Notes
Sugar-glazed Ham	Honeybaked Ham Co.	M-Sat. 10-7 Sun. 10-4	877-5527	Check OK
Curried Hot Fruit	Silver Palate	M-F 9-8 S-Sun. 8-5	721-4630	
Brioche	Amsterdam Patisserie	M-Sat. 8-6 Sun. 9-5	847-5541	Visa Only
Spinach Quiche	Maison Roberd	M-Sat. 10-6 Sun. 12-5	656-1655	Park—lot on Crestwood
Fresh Orange Juice	Korean Grocer	7 days week 8-10		No Cards, Cash Only
Fresh Coffee	Coffee Connection	M-F 8-6 S-Sun. 10-4	426-3751	

Accessories for the "Well-Dressed" Bar

Checklist:

- Ice bucket, with tongs or spoon

- 2-oz. jigger (marked for each ounce)

- Bottle opener and cork-screw

- Glass or silver, not metal, stirrer (metal gives some drinks an unpleasant taste)

- Plate or bowl for cut lemons and limes (non-silver)

- Small board for cutting lemons and limes

- Serrated-edge cocktail knife (some have double-pronged tips for spearing cocktail olives or onions)

- Lemon peeler

- Clean white towel, preferably linen

- Tray for serving drinks

- Cocktail napkins

- Water pitcher

- Seltzer charger

- Crystal decanters

Miscellaneous:

- Tub or cooler for chilling wine and beer for a large party

- Glass swizzle sticks

- Bottle stoppers

- Champagne corker

- Bowl for salt or sugar

Random sampling of to-do's that might appear on a

24-HOUR PRE-PARTY CHECKLIST

Whenever possible, move items from this "last-minute" checklist to the "plan ahead checklist"—

❑ Clear kitchen counters

❑ Edit and organize fridge

❑ Empty and run dishwasher

❑ Chill wine/beer/champagne

❑ Fill salt and peppers

❑ Prepare sugar and creamer

❑ Take cheeses out of fridge

❑ Cut lemons and limes

❑ Arrange after-dinner mints

❑ Build the fire

❑ If raining or snowing, put indoor mat at guest entrance

❑ Put out holder for umbrellas

❑ Empty hangers in coat closet

❑ Put guest towels, new soap and toilet paper in guest bath

❑ Remove furniture pet covers

❑ Put out serving dishes and utensils (label each for caterer)

❑ Put out new candles/ votives

❑ Put out ashtrays

❑ Set table

❑ Make out place cards

❑ Re-check seating chart for last minute changes

❑ Arrange flowers

❑ Have music set to go

❑ Write notes to sitter

❑ Pick up sitter

❑ Feed cat/dog and put in non-party location

❑ Empty trash

❑ "Walk Through"; Practice order of events and logistics

PLAN AHEAD CHECKLIST

An incomplete listing of party preparations, touching on a variety of entertaining formats. All should be completed in the week before the party.

Use this as a memory jogger when compiling your own list.

❏ Calculate time needed for shopping, cooking, house cleaning, flower arranging.

❏ Clean candle holders and votives.

❏ Polish silver (how about silver picture frames, top to wine carafe, etc.).

❏ Sharpen kitchen knives.

❏ Polish brass on front door. ·

❏ Bag own ice from freezer trays/ice makers in ice bucket size quantities.

❏ Buy place cards.

❏ Wrap party favors.

❏ Make space in hall closet for coats/replenish hangers.

❏ Pull out collapsible coat rack.

❏ Check glasses and plates. Wash if necessary.

❏ Rent minibus/borrow station wagon for ferrying people.

❏ Get petty cash for staff payments, tips, emergencies.

❏ Line up someone to open door (apartment lobby/hallway main entrance).

❏ Line up someone to drive "shuttle."

❏ Arrange seating chart.

❏ Check flower arranging staples and equipment.

❏ Clean or iron attire for evening.

❏ Check liquor and wine supply/cocktail napkins.

❏ Telephone guests.

❏ Buy, address, stamp, mail invitations.

❏ Check and/or iron table skirt, place mats, napkins.

❏ Call/track down special or seasonal food items.

❏ Review grounds with yard service.

❏ Schedule pool cleaning for day before party.

Example: Catered Cocktail Buffet for 24
(This doesn't presume every detail or contingency, but it does give an overview of how to organize a special event versus a Sunday night pot luck supper.)

WEEK 6:

Format budget.
Reserve caterer, bartender, any support staff.
Compile guest list.
Discuss theme and decorations with florist and/or designer.
Call babysitter.
Design and order printed invitations (order envelopes sent immediately).
Order personalized cocktail napkins, matches, place cards, menu cards.
Reserve calligrapher/addresser.
Research entertainment and musical options.

WEEK 5:

Buy fabric/deliver to workroom for table skirt fabrication, napkins, etc.
Discuss/design menu—review kitchen facilities with caterer.
Deliver envelopes to addresser.
Decide on evening's outfit — purchase and/or check for alterations.
Meet with florist — order special or hard-to-get flowers if necessary.

WEEK 4:

Test sample caterer's menu and approve.
Order any special wines or champagnes.
Determine serving and entertaining pieces — refurbish or replace where needed.
Place order with party rental service.
Purchase special stamps/mail invitations.
Start shopping for party favors.
Meet with musical group to discuss style, special requests, list of their specific needs; check on sufficient electricity for their sound systems.
Send rugs out to be cleaned.

Week 3:

Check linens; launder, iron if needed.

Arrange to rent van, borrow station wagon to ferry guests up driveway.

Meet with yard service to review major maintenance.

Week 2:

Major house cleanup.

Monitor acceptances and regrets.

Make decision regarding alternates to guest list.

Pick up tableskirts and napkins.

Week 1:

Minor house clean-up.

Floors waxed/windows washed.

Clean and polish brass and silver.

Add extra kitchen supplies and food staples to shopping list.

Call guests who have not responded.

Order wine, liquors, mixers.

Day 2:

Clean pool.

Pick up or arrange for someone to accept delivery of wine, liquor, mixers.

Pick up cash at bank.

Set up tables with cloths.

Check coat closet.

Arrange flowers.

Write place cards.

Day 1:

Water, last-minute yard clean-up.

Party rental delivery.

Floral decorations delivery.

Arrange seating.

Caterer, bartender arrive 2 hours early/bring ice.

Set three tables and buffet sideboard.

Put out torchieres in garden and along driveway.

Pick up station wagon to shuttle guests.

Coordinate with arriving musicians.

KITCHEN NOTES

Sample instructions for Caterer and Staff

- Hand wash: any plates with gold decoration.

- Hand wash: champagne flutes.

- Hand wash: ivy-bordered dessert plates.

- Do not put knives in dishwasher
  (exception; stainless steel).

- When putting glasses away: do not let them touch,
  do not stack or turn upside down.

- Use rubber grid mat in sink when washing all crystal.

- Do not let tapered bottom cocktail glasses touch in
  dishwasher.

- Empty silver salt shakers.

When the party is over, DON'T FORGET to:

- ❏ Turn off stereo/CD/tape player.

- ❏ Close windows.

- ❏ Or open windows to air the room.

- ❏ Make sure the fire is out.

- ❏ Secure the house; turn on alarm system.

- ❏ Rinse wine glasses and silver food dishes.

- ❏ Let the dog outside, take home the babysitter, pick up the children.

- ❏ Make sure the stove and other appliances are turned off.

- ❏ Start the dishwasher.

- ❏ Put out the garbage (if there is no chance of animals tearing it open).

- ❏ Pay and tip staff.

- ❏ Recount silver (when necessary).

- ❏ Arrange to have an inebriated guest driven home; or drive yourself.

- ❏ Do a quick check for fresh spills or stains.

- ❏ Empty silver pieces filled with salt, vinegar, lemon juice, anything acidic.

- ❏ Empty ashtrays, wipe with disposable cloths moistened with household cleaner.

- ❏ Drink a big glass of water and take two aspirin.

Next Day:

Assess wear and tear damage and take immediate remedial action. Tip the garbage man if trash is excessive.

FORMAL TABLE-SETTING GUIDELINES

I've chosen a 5-course dinner because it requires so much table-top paraphernalia, and therefore a thorough checklist to ease party planning. Prepare a checklist for your favorite style of entertaining and see what a time-saver it will prove to be.

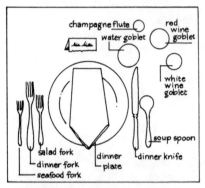

First course *(seafood appetizer) with seafood dish and liner plate. Both will be removed, but the service plate will remain to receive the second course.*

Second course *with soup bowl and liner plate in place. Once the course is finished, both will be removed along with the service plate. A dinner plate is then put down before the entrée is served.*

FORMAL TABLE-SETTING GUIDELINES

◊   Silver is always placed left and right so the diner works from the outside in toward the plate in choosing his flatware.

◊   Goblets and glasses are also placed in the progression of usage and removed with the course to which they pertain. The water goblet remains through dessert.

◊   When coffee is served away from the table, a teaspoon is not used in the place setting.

◊   Bread and butter plates are not used. Rolls are placed directly on the folded napkin atop a service plate; or on the tablecloth, above the forks, if passed to a guest.

Sample Five-course Menu

seafood appetizer (with white wine) ❦ *soup*
entrée (with red wine) ❦ *salad* ❦ *dessert (with champagne)*

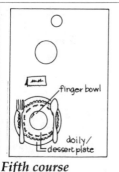

Third course *with service plate removed and dinner plate set to receive entrée.*

Fourth course *with salad plate replacing dinner plate. Note that only the salad fork remains, all other flatware having been removed with three earlier courses.*

Fifth course *with finger bowl and doily on dessert plate; dessert fork and spoon on plate.*
Finger bowl, with doily, is removed by diner and placed on table to upper left; fork and spoon are placed on table to left and right of dessert plate. Dessert **is then served.**

SAMPLE PARTY NECESSITIES CHECKLIST

❏ service (or place) plate
❏ soup bowl and liner plate
❏ seafood dish and liner plate
❏ dinner plate
❏ salad plate
❏ dessert plate
❏ finger bowls
❏ soup spoon
❏ seafood fork
❏ dinner knife and fork
❏ salad fork
❏ dessert fork and spoon
❏ water goblet

❏ red wine goblet
❏ white wine goblet
❏ champagne flute
❏ demitasse cup and saucer
❏ demitasse spoons
❏ serving dishes
❏ trays
❏ serving flatware
❏ coffee pot, cream, sugar and tray
❏ salt cellar or shaker
❏ salt spoon
❏ pepper shaker
❏ wine carafe
❏ wine coaster
❏ brandy decanter and brandy snifters
❏ liqueur glasses

❏ tablecloth, or table runner and place mats
❏ napkins
❏ candlesticks

Miscellaneous
❏ candles
❏ bud vases
❏ place cards
❏ menu cards and holders
❏ doilies
❏ seating chart
❏ after-dinner chocolates
❏ linen guest towels and cocktail napkins

Sample
Three-course Menu 1

soup

❦

fish entrée
(with white wine)
with salad

❦

dessert

All the flatware that is needed for the 3 courses is placed on the table, including dessert fork and spoon and teaspoon for coffee.

The soup bowl and its plate will be replaced by the dinner plate and then the dessert dish/plate.

The informal place setting, pictured, takes advantage of the flexibility afforded today's host in setting an attractive and serviceable table.

Today, china need not match, glass can be mixed with pottery and wood, and oversized or irregular shapes can highlight any course (i.e., glass crescent in lieu of the more traditional salad plate, pictured). An all-purpose wine glass is an additional convenience that can be used for both red and white wines.

Sample Three-course Menu 2

lamb ❦ salad with cheese ❦ dessert

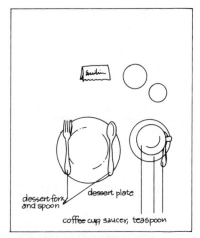

Another setting for an informal dinner whose menu is lamb with red wine, salad with cheese, dessert. The salad is served after the entrée as its own course. When cheese is served with salad, it is necessary to include a salad knife. The glasses remain through all 3 courses and the dessert is brought in separately, as pictured.

After the salad plate is removed, the dessert plate with fork and spoon as positioned is brought in. The fork and spoon should then be placed on the table by the diner before the dessert is served. At an informal dinner, the coffee cup and saucer with spoon are also brought.

PARTY NECESSITIES CHECKLIST
3-course seated luncheon—soup, fish entrée with salad, dessert

- ❑ salad plate
- ❑ luncheon plate
- ❑ dessert plate & dish
- ❑ soup spoon
- ❑ fish fork & knife
- ❑ salad fork
- ❑ dessert fork & spoon
- ❑ teaspoon
- ❑ water goblet
- ❑ all-purpose wine goblet
- ❑ coffee cup & saucer
- ❑ serving dishes
- ❑ serving flatware
- ❑ serving trays

- ❑ coffee pot
- ❑ cream, sugar & tray
- ❑ salt & pepper shakers
- ❑ wine carafe
- ❑ wine coaster

Miscellaneous
- ❑ tablecloth or place mats
- ❑ napkins
- ❑ place cards
- ❑ bud vases
- ❑ linen guest towels
- ❑ cocktail napkins

Quick Tricks with Sheets

✄ A king FLAT sheet (102" x 108") is all you need to create an instant floor length tablecloth for round tables up to 48" in diameter.

✄ For 54" diameter tables, use a king FLAT sheet with an additional 6" ruffle cut from a twin sheet.

✄ For a decorative touch, top your new tablecloth with a square overlay made from standard width fabric (54") or accent with a large decorative shawl.

How to Cut Round Tablecloths from FLAT KING SHEETS:

You will need:

PARDEE TIP	
Working on a carpeted surface makes this process easier.	1 King sheet (102" x 108") 1 ball of string 1 felt tip pen 1 pair of scissors 1 push pin

For this exercise, a 48" tabletop is being used as an example. The finished circle is equal to diameter of table   48"
plus 2 x table height of 30"   + 60"

                                                108" circle

1. Begin with sheet opened fully and pattern-side up.
2. Fold the longer side in half, giving you a 102" x 54" rectangle. The sheet will now be inside out.
3. Determine radius of table skirt (RADIUS = $\frac{\text{DIAMETER}}{2}$ or $\frac{108"}{2}$ = 54")
4. Measure out the radius (54") on a length of string, leaving surplus string to attach to the push pin and the felt tip pen.
5. Tie a string knot around the push pin and the other end around the marking pen.
6. Center push pin on *folded* edge of sheet and secure by sticking pin into carpet.
7. Making sure that string length remains equal to the radius (54"), start at one folded sheet edge and mark a full arc around sheet to other folded edge.
8. Leaving sheet folded, cut the half circle with scissors (taking care not to cut the carpet).

Making Topiaries

You will need:
- 1 flowerpot or other sturdy decorative container
- 1 dowel or straight tree limb
- 1 green styrofoam ball or florist's circular green foam short floral sticks with wiring at one end
- plastic flower picks to fill with water
- fresh dried blossoms, leaves, nuts
- sheet moss

1. Fill container with plaster of paris, mixed with water per package instructions.

2. Press dowel or limb into mixture as it is hardening. This represents the tree trunk.

3. If choosing styrofoam for the treetop ball: cover the sheet moss by wrapping and encircling with transparent fishing line. Wire material onto short wooden sticks; push sticks directly into ball.

4. If using green foam for the topiary: soak with water, form into a round shape, press fresh flower stems directly into foam.
   or
   Plunge flower stems into water-filled plastic flower picks and push picks into foam.

5. Complete with bow and streamers around trunk; cover plaster of paris area with moss.